Jews, Germany, Memory

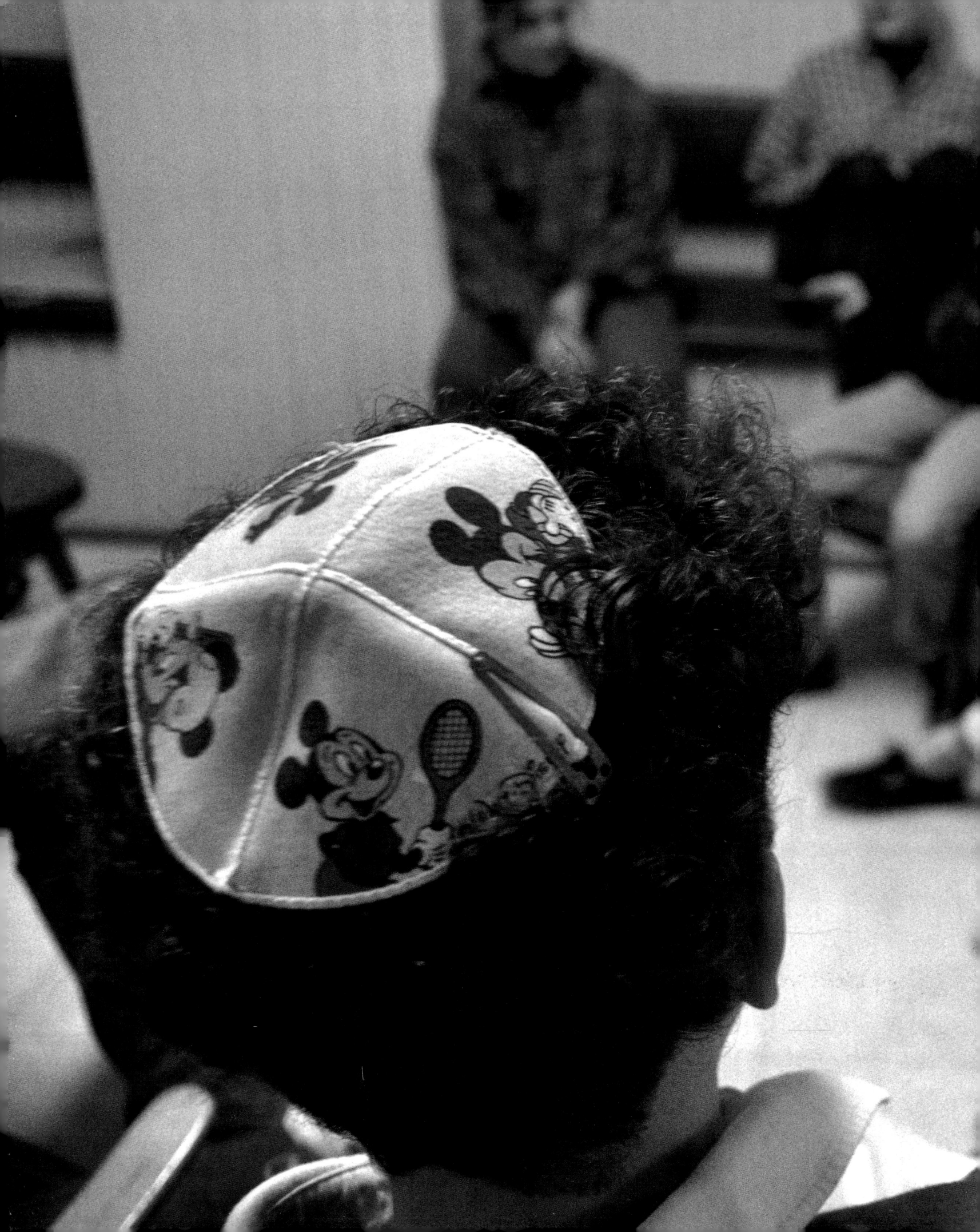

Meeting at the Youth Club. Jewish community center Cologne.
November 1993.

Jews Germany Memory

A Contemporary Portrait

Edward Serotta

Nicolai

© 1996 Nicolaische Verlagsbuchhandlung
Beuermann GmbH, Berlin

Design: Dorén + Köster, Berlin
Typesetting: Mega-Satz-Service, Berlin
Lithos: Imago Publishing Ltd., Oxfordshire
Printing: Passavia Druckerei GmbH, Passau
Binding: Kunst- und Verlagsbuchbinderei GmbH, Leipzig
Illustration page 40: Survivors of the Shoah Visual History Foundation

CENTRAL EUROPE CENTER
For Research & Documentation

This book has been published in conjunction
with the Jüdische Kulturtage Berlin 1996.

Dedication

When I moved to Berlin in 1991, I took an apartment on Bruchsaler Strasse, a short cobblestone street of uninteresting buildings, enormous shade trees, a couple of decent restaurants, and neighbors who, when the sun was bright and the weather warm, nodded their friendly greetings. The majority of the residents seem to be under fifty years old.

Over the years, as I walked, drove and biked my way up and down this street, I began to wonder about other Jewish residents. The Berlin Jewish community registers no other members on Bruchsaler Strasse except me, but Hermann Simon, director of the Centrum Judaicum Museum, faxed me a list of Jews who once lived on this street. I dedicate this book to them—the lives behind the numbers on the doors.

Martha Ullmann lived at number 6. When she was sixty-six years old in 1943, she was deported to Auschwitz. She did not return.

At number 8, Charlotte Wegner and her son Horst lived. They managed to leave this street in 1939 on their own accord and their fate is unknown.

At number 11, Paul and Pauline Boehme lived. Shortly before being deported to Theresienstadt, Paul died. Pauline, at seventy-three years old, was transported there, and survived.

Felix Rosenthal and his two young sons, Kurt and Carl-Heinz, lived in number 15. They fled Germany for Shanghai.

From my living room window I can look down the street to number 12. Several Jewish families were registered at that address. Perhaps they were forced to move in together by the authorities; it is possible they were an extended family and clung together out of fear. In any case, between August 1942 and March 1943, sixty-eight year old Dr Hugo Schwabach was deported from this address to Theresienstadt and fifty-eight year old Elsa Rosenhain was also sent to Theresienstadt. Herbert and Gertrud Krisch, both in their thirties, were shipped to Auschwitz, as was the seventy-four year old Max Levy. Hertha Markus and her husband Klaus, in their forties, also were transported to Auschwitz. Of these, only Max Levy was alive in 1945.

At number 11, Werner Rosenthal and his son Klaus lived. They survived the war and continued to live in this neighborhood after the war.

Edward Serotta, August 1996

Contents

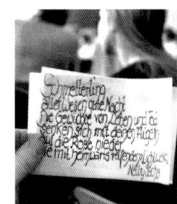

To Auschwitz with Germans
November 1989

The motorcade of police cars, Mercedes limousines and buses cut its way across southern Poland toward the Cracow airport. Inside the first bus were forty German photographers and reporters who had just accompanied the West German Chancellor, Helmut Kohl, on his first visit to Auschwitz and Birkenau.

Except for the whine of tires on the asphalt, there was total silence in that bus. Minutes before, Heinz Galinski, the seventy-seven years old Chairman of the Central Council of Jews in Germany, had faced the German head of state and recounted how forty-six years ago, he, his first wife and his mother had been brought to this place. He spoke of the very last time he saw them as they were separated from each other on the ramp next to the railroad tracks. Heinz Galinski spent the next twenty-six months in work camps and on death marches. His wife and mother were gassed – right there. He told his story in flat, cold cadences that seemed to pierce the German dignitaries like arrows. Then Menachem Joskowicz, Poland's sole rabbi, stood next to Galinski and recited Kaddish, the Jewish prayer for the dead. As he prayed, he closed his

Auschwitz. November 1989.

eyes and his hands grabbed at the air before him, as if he were beseeching those around him to feel the power of the words. When he finished, for a long, pregnant, painful moment, no one moved, nothing stirred. Suddenly, everyone headed quickly toward the waiting cars and buses.

It was clear how much the experience had shaken the photographers. They cleaned lenses, rewound films, and looked anywhere but at each other. I was the only non-German, and the only Jew, on that bus. Back at Birkenau, I had been the only one who had covered his head with a yarmulke during Kaddish.

I had gone to Auschwitz with the Germans in hope of finding some usable pictures for my first book on Jews in Central Europe, *Out of the Shadows*, a project I had been working on for nearly four years. Living in Budapest since 1988 and roaming the whole of what was then the East Bloc, I interviewed and photographed scores of Holocaust survivors. Speaking with them in city and village alike, I spent a great deal of time in a Jewish world that existed only in their memories, a world which had been destroyed primarily by Germans. In time, I developed (and still maintain) a great respect for those who rebuilt Jewish communities in these

Auschwitz. November 1989.

lands after the Holocaust, but as my respect for them grew, I found the reverse was true of my feelings for the land, the language and the people who had originated, organized and perpetrated that unspeakable crime. Until this moment, I had not spoken with anyone on the bus, and no one had said anything to me. As Galinski's words echoed in my own ears, I figured that was just fine. Suddenly, a young photographer turned to me. "That's the first time I've ever been to such a place!" he said, nearly blurting out the words in English. "I never learned anything about the Holocaust in school and my teachers refused to discuss it." When he saw the surprised look on my face, he hastily added, "I saw you wearing that little cap at Birkenau when the rabbi prayed. You are – Israeli?"

Taken aback, I shook my head. I stammered that I was an American. "But Jewish," I added.

Another photographer turned to me. "When we asked our teacher about the Holocaust, she said all we have to know is that everything the Nazis did was horrible, and we should do the opposite," he said softly. "Then she started crying so we didn't push it any more."

Another came and sat down. "Crying has always been a good way to stop the children from asking about the war," he said, "especially at home." Heads nodded in agreement.

It seemed everyone wanted to say something, but the words, in English or German, weren't coming. Then one young man began slowly. "Well our teacher made us learn – by memory – 'Todesfuge,' by Paul Celan. Death Fugue in English. Do you know it?"

I said I didn't.

"Well I still do. I even brought a copy with me and I read it this morning." And repeating from memory, he recited the entire poem, finishing with the final, chilling lines:

Black milk of daybreak we drink you at night / we drink you at noon death is a master from Germany / we drink you at sundown and in the morning we drink and we drink you / death is a master from Germany his eyes are blue / he strikes you with leaden bullets his aim is true / a man lives in the house your golden hair Margarete / he sets his pack on to us he grants us a grave in the air he plays with

the serpents and daydreams death is a master from Germany / your golden hair Margarete / your ashen hair Shulamith (translation by Michael Hamburger)

The press bus rolled on. No one said a word. Finally, this sandy-haired young man, whose name I never learned, looked up. Staring at me, he said, "So I'm German." He paused, and as if to explain something, he added, "and twenty-four years old. Bloody, bloody Germany. Bloody, bloody me."

I don't think I had ever felt so moved, so confused, in my life: The only Jew in a bus full of young Germans who had just confronted this greatest of all crimes, carried out in their country's name, carried out in the language their mothers spoke to them. They were no more guilty of this crime than I was a victim of it. But the connection: German and Jew, was clearly there. Still, I could add no words, and I remained silent.

Minutes later we stepped off the bus at the Cracow airport. As if we were all embarrassed by the sudden rush of emotion, we bade each other hasty good-byes. They filed out toward a massive Boeing with *Luftwaffe* written across its fuselage. I boarded a flimsy-looking Tupelov bound for Warsaw.

By the time their plane was pulling up to its gate at the Bonn/Cologne airport, I was walking through the sooty Polish capital, past the remains of the Warsaw ghetto to the flat I was renting that month. Inside, as I listened for the tea kettle to hiss, I marked each roll of film: Auschwitz, Auschwitz, Birkenau, Birkenau. I dropped them into a bag with my German press pass to Auschwitz. I had no radio, no television, and I wished to God I wasn't alone. But I was alone, and as I felt the weight of being in a Jewish quarter of a city almost wholly bereft of Jews, I asked myself, how does one get over, get around, the Holocaust?

One doesn't, I thought as I poured the tea. One never does. Not the Jews, who lost an entire civilization to the Nazis' murderous ideology. Not the Germans. For I believe when you take a life, you do just that. The life you take is forever with you; even after your own death you are linked as one. Now and forever, Germany will be known as the land of poets and thinkers, *(Dichter und Denker)* just as it always was. But it is also the land of mass murder-

Helmut Kohl, chancellor of what was then West Germany, at the Birkenau death camp with Heinz Galinski, chairman of the Central Council of Jews in Germany. November 1989.

ers. For Nazis are now as intrinsic a part of German culture as Goethe's poetry, Bavarian lederhosen and the architecture of Schinkel.

Still, I kept thinking about the guys on the bus, now home in Germany with wives, girlfriends and mothers. Germany: where evil lay. Did it still? Were the people I was just with different than those who refused to talk about the past; those who carried out the awful deeds; those who did nothing but mutely look on? Had today's Germans learned from, and about, the Holocaust? More than a few of my fellow Jews in America and Israel had an easy answer: No. But I wasn't sure. And I knew then I would have to find out for myself.

From that night on I have been intrigued, not so much with the evil done, but with evil's aftermath and its legacy. That is why I had to make this book.

Seeking Stones

On the day I moved to Berlin in July 1991, I bought a bicycle. The next day, on a mild and leafy Sunday, I left the house early, map in hand. I pedaled past the office blocks of west Berlin and through the Brandenburg Gate where the wall had once stood, past Adolf Hitler's grave. Pausing to consult the map, I veered off the avenue, Unter den Linden, and into the Spandauer Vorstadt, Ber-

Grave of Moses Mendelssohn, Grosse Hamburger Strasse, Berlin. July 1991.

lin's first Jewish quarter. After a few minutes, I found the address I was looking for on Grosse Hamburger Strasse, the oldest Jewish cemetery in the city.

I was indulging a habit I'd started a decade ago when I began working in Central Europe. Whenever I arrived in a city I didn't know, I would first visit the Jewish cemetery to get a feel for the community. Cemeteries are reflections of the societies that build them, and throughout Central Europe, Jewish cemeteries bear witness to the ebb and flow of empire, the rise of 19th century nationalism, the optimism of the turn-of-the-century, the disruption of the First World War, then the Holocaust and what came after. Berlin's resting places would

During the Cold War, Adolf Hitler's bunker, near Leipziger Strasse, sat in no-man's-land at the edge of East Berlin. This entire site is now covered with construction sites. July 1991.

prove no different, I thought. There are four cemeteries scattered across one of the largest and most sprawling cities in Europe; this would be a full day's ride.

Berlin's first Jewish cemetery stands wedged into a pocket-sized plot surrounded by crumbling buildings. No signs mark it. The Nazis destroyed the gravestones so the space is now just a park where neighbors walk their dogs. I locked my bike and walked around under the trees. Just one stone had been resurrected: that of Moses Mendelssohn.

This cemetery was consecrated in 1672, one year after Jews had been given permission to settle in Berlin. Not quite fifty Jewish residents were registered in a city which then had a total population of 8,150, and the Spandauer Vorstadt stood outside the city walls. When the last of the cemetery's 2,700 graves was filled one hundered fifty-five years later in 1827, 4,900 Jews lived in a Berlin of 230,000. By then there were no more city walls and the Spandauer Vorstadt had been swallowed by a rapidly growing city.

By that time, Prussia was a world power. Revolution had come and gone in France; so had Napoleon. And as militaristic as Prussia's rulers were, they were grudgingly tolerant. Jews enjoyed freedoms in Berlin as in no other north German city, and the Prussian capital was also known for accepting Poles and Huguenot Frenchmen and others on the run.

Moses Mendelssohn was the dominant Jewish figure of his age in Central Europe. Born in Dessau in 1729, he was fourteen when he came to Berlin and remained there until he died in 1786. Although he was a philosopher influenced by the Enlightenment, Moses Mendelssohn is best remembered for the way he lived his life, as a Jew coming to terms with his environment. Here was a man who had been born into an orthodox Jewish world, yet in time he encouraged Jews to adopt the patterns of the society in which they lived. He embraced German culture and the German language, and felt Judaism was strong enough to withstand the onslaught of Christian secular society. It was for him, but not for his children. They converted out of the religion, and Moses Mendelssohn was the last Jew of his line. His tombstone, all alone in that leafy public park, spoke volumes.

The sound of a nearby tram scraping along in its tracks brought me back to my task. I pedaled away uphill, onto tree-lined Schönhauser Allee where I stopped before a high brick wall. Here an iron gate opened onto a jumble of 22,500 tombstones, a Jewish cemetery the Nazis had never bothered to destroy. As a caretaker in dusty overalls came shuffling out with a key, I reached into my pocket for a yarmulke to cover my head.

Community leaders probably felt this five hectare site, which they opened in 1827, would last them into the next century. They were wrong. Some 10,000 Jews lived in Berlin in the early 1850s; in less than twenty years there were 36,000. By 1880, except for family-reserved plots, this cemetery had nearly filled. Some stones were written solely in Hebrew, but many had German inscribed beneath. Jews were beginning to follow Mendelssohn's advice out of the ghetto.

As Berlin rapidly became one of Europe's most industrialized cities, Jews from Prussia's Polish-occupied territories and from lands even farther to the east gravitated to this boom-town. Tens of thousands settled in the Scheunenviertel, which became an insular, Yiddish world like the one they had left, geographically, behind. But an increasing number of Jews eagerly seized the opportunities offered by Berlin and plunged into the worlds of business and culture. Soon, a fifth of Berlin's newspapers were owned by Jews. The largest armaments manufactury belonged to a Jewish family, and sixteen percent of all lawyers were Jewish. The vast array of gravestones before me mirrored this world. The wealthy had built impressive memorials along the walls and in special rows. The middle class, the orthodox and poor bought modest stones and filled the interior spaces. But the condition of the graves told another story. With no families left alive, or in Germany, to care for the plots, Schönhauser Allee was nearly choked in weeds and bushes. Overhead, century-old elms formed a solid canopy.

During the years Berlin Jews laid their loved ones to rest here, Chancellor Bismarck went to war with Austria to establish Prussian hegemony in the German world. In 1870, he went to war with France. That enabled him to forge the disparate German principalities, kingdoms, duchies and states into a single empire, and for the first time in the modern age, Germany was united.

Here in this overgrown, all but abandoned cemetery, I found a simple and elegant granite memorial that signified all of this. It belonged to Gerson von Bleichröder. Under this stone rests Otto von Bismarck's banker, the man who helped finance the iron chancellor's wars, handled his personal accounts and remained a personal confidant throughout his life. In 1878, the relationship between Bleichröder and Bismarck was so strong that the banker asked the politician to intercede at the Congress of Berlin to put pressure on Romania to ease the plight of its impoverished Jewish population. (Gold and Iron: Bismarck, Bleichröder and the building of the German Empire, by Fritz Stern. New York 1977)

Gerson von Bleichröder was the first Jew in Germany to be raised to the nobility and the bank that bore his name became powerful and well-respected at home and abroad. Governments and ministries the world over came to the firm for underwriting. But although he was one of the richest men in this powerful new empire, he was not the first Jew to learn that money does not always buy power. With slurs and slander peppering his name and reputation, he felt the rising

Jew-hatred that in the latter part of the nineteenth century grew to be perfectly respectable. Indeed, by 1879, when the highly regarded historian Heinrich von Treitschke wrote that "the Jews are our misfortune", anti-Semitism had become downright patriotic throughout Germany.

Schönhauser Allee is now lined with apartment houses that sag from years of communist-era neglect. It borders Prenzlauer Berg, a district that historically was socialist and working class, but since German unification has become trendy and chic. I rode through its lumpy streets and crossed over to Greifswalder Strasse. I turned right on Herbert-Baum-Strasse where massive wrought iron gates guard the entrance to the Weissensee Jewish cemetery, called by some (in Berlin at least) the largest Jewish cemetery in all Europe.

"Now we've got it right", community leaders must have thought as they swung open the gates in 1880. An elegant ceremonial hall looms behind a manicured garden. Arched porticos stretch outwards, lined with white wooden benches. The cemetery itself is laid out over forty hectares, criss-crossed with cobbled, tree-lined lands.

By the turn of the century, the Jewish population was still swelling, not only here in Berlin, where over 150,000 Jews lived in 1910, but throughout Germany as well. As the economy grew, German Jews found an increasing number of doors open to them. Although high society remained largely closed – unless they converted – Jews became prominent in business, science, education and the arts. They took enormous pride in being German. When they were asked to aid their Fatherland during the First World War, 90,000 Jewish men enlisted and 12,000 died fighting. There, in the heart of Weissensee, lies a soldiers memorial for "our fallen sons." In other countries, dying for one's country is called the supreme sacrifice. Here it turned out to be the supreme irony.

During that war, Alfred Ballin, a Jew, was an adviser to the Kaiser on naval matters. Walter Rathenau helped finance the armaments industry. Fritz Haber, who went on to win the Nobel Prize, invented nerve gas for the German Army. And while Ballin committed suicide upon hearing of Germany's surrender in 1918, Rathenau was shot to death by rightists while serving as foreign minister in 1923. Haber converted out of Judaism, but when the Nazis told him to fire Jewish scientists in his institute in 1933, he refused, left for Switzerland, and died a broken man.

Even on the hottest days, one can feel a chill in Weissensee. Here, etched in stone, are the names that brightened Berlin and still do: Hermann Tietz of the Hertie Department stores; Adolf Jandorf, who created Tietz's competition, the massive *KaDeWe*; Leopold Ullstein, the publishing baron; Berthold Kempinski of restaurant and hotel fame. The rich and the powerful – newspaper publishers and factory owners, bankers and businessmen, landlords and lawyers – are all here. Their tombstones and family mausoleums say a great deal of how proud they must have been, and below their names, their titles boast of how far German Jewry had traveled from the ghetto: commercial adviser to the Throne of Prussia, member of the Finance Committee of the city of Berlin, Judge, Attorney-at-law, city councilman.

And in the vast plots behind these stone monuments are the tens upon tens of thousands of more modest stones: the shop owners, professionals, workers and crafts-men and women who put their backs into Germany's economy, year after year, decade after decade. They saved, they planned, they dreamed: in Germany.

All for naught. The Nazis came and the Jewish life that had been building steadily on German soil for hundreds of years came to a brutal end. Now this proudest of cemeteries, this forty hectare monument to the golden age of German Jewry, lay nearly submerged in ivy. Gravestones had toppled and some lay submerged in vegetation. And I saw that more than a few family plots had never been filled. Tearing away the weeds I saw why: single words were engraved in stone – Treblinka, Theresienstadt, Buchenwald.

Weissensee's fifty year history ended with the Second World War. By then, 115,000 Jews had been buried here. Oddly enough, the Nazis never got around to destroying it as the place was simply so huge. There were even a few war-time burials. In the Nazis' perverse obsession with order, terminally-ill Jews were not deported from the city's Jewish hospital, although all the doctors, administrators and nurses were. When the patients died, they

Grave of Gerson von Bleichröder, Jewish cemetery Schönhauser Allee, Berlin. July 1991.

Detail: Weissensee Jewish cemetery. July 1991.

were buried here in Weissensee and legends even abound that during the war a few Jews hid for months at a time among the tombs.

The Cold War placed Weissensee in Communist East Berlin, and for nearly five decades the great cemetery was cut off from the small West Berlin Jewish community. Slipping slowly into disrepair, a vandal or two climbed over the walls to chip away brass lettering from the once-proud, now defenseless dead, or cart away the heavy chains and the bronze plaques. Only a few hundred Jews lived in East Berlin; a small cluster of post-war tombstones huddled behind the ceremonial hall honor their dead.

I walked for hours, stopping on occasion to take pictures in this vast, verdant necropolis. It was mid-afternoon before I found the elderly caretaker and asked him to point out on a map the cemetery that the West Berlin community had been using during the Cold War. It was ten kilometers due west and I hurriedly stowed my cameras and jumped on my bike for the trek across town.

Monument to Jewish soldiers killed in World War I. Jewish cemetery Weissensee. July 1991.

As it was, I pedaled up to the modest gate of the Heerstrasse Jewish cemetery just as the guard was closing it for the day. He was a patient man though, and allowed me time for a visit.

The contrast with the three cemeteries I had visited in the course of the day was striking. Here was a prim little burial ground, where sprinklers hiss in summer and nine workers keep the weeds well away from the 4,600 tombs. The first grave was dug in 1955, but the most prominent markers commemorate unnamed Jews taken to death camps during the war. There are no huge marble monuments here, no sense of optimism of being a Jew in Germany. Indeed, I asked myself as I stepped over the white gravel, was there even such a thing today as a German Jew? Most Jews here seemed to say no. Many Germans said yes. "So now we can finally, really be German Jews," the Berlin-born Gershom Scholem wrote bitterly after the Holocaust from his home in Jerusalem. "It is as if we have been awarded some posthumous prize."

Auschwitz monument at the Jewish cemetery Heerstrasse. July 1991.

22

Jewish was our religion,
German is what we were

Expulsion

In Berlin after the First World War, Alfred and Henny Alexander had every reason to believe their children, Elsie, Hans and Paul, would enjoy the world their parents were building for them. Forty miles to the east, in Küstrin, Arthur and Henrietta Hirschberg worked and saved so that their son Louis could study law (just as he dreamt of doing). And in Krefeld on the Rhine, Carl and Martha Meyer had every confidence that their hard work would provide a solid future for their daughters Ruth and Ilsa.

The Kaiser abdicated, Weimar wobbled and anti-Semitism grew stronger. But these families held their ground in Germany, and not without reason. The Alexanders, Hirschbergs and Meyers had lived on German soil for generations. Arthur Hirschberg had been wounded fighting for Germany in the First World War, and Alfred Alexander had been decorated with the Iron Cross.

History, wearing a brown shirt, was about to stand in their way. It would send their children fleeing for their lives. The Alexanders and Meyers ran after them. Arthur and Henrietta Hirschberg, relieved that their son had made it to safety, did not look for a way out until it was too late, and in the end, they waited at home for the knock on the door that was sure to come.

Today the Berlin street where the Alexanders lived is called Bundes Allee (Federal Avenue). It is a drab, nondescript thoroughfare lined with anony-

mous blocks put up after Allied bombs leveled much of it between 1943-1945. At the turn of the century, it was called Kaiser Allee and handsome entrance ways were braced by marble pillars. Doormen stood inside paneled lobbies and announced guests to uniformed maids inside. Elsie, Hans and Paul Alexander were of this world. Elsie was born in 1913; the twins followed four years later.

"Our father's medical practice was attached to our living quarters," the spry, eighty-two years old Elsie said over coffee in her London apartment in 1995. "All together we had twenty-two rooms, eight of which belonged to the clinic." A full-time cook did the marketing and tended the kitchen. Two full-time maids, Ilsa and Hilda, kept the house spotless. The washing and ironing were done by part-timers who bustled in and out with laundry baskets. Anna, the governess, looked after Hans and Paul, while Robert, the chauffeur, made sure the Mercedes limousine and Dr. Alexander's Adler were always tuned and polished. When summer came to Brandenburg, the Alexanders had their possessions packed and moved down to their lake-side cottage south of town. At the end of the hot season, while the parents holidayed alone in Italy and Elsie went off with friends Anna took Hans and Paul home to her village, where they played in the fields and helped out on the family farm.

They led privileged lives, and the Alexanders knew it. "Back then, there was a difference between German Jews and Jewish Germans," Elsie said. "We were the latter. In our family, Jewish was our religion. German was what we were." She paused and then formed the next word slowly and sternly. "Were." She stood up and went to the win-

Just after Adolf Hitler's election in 1933, the national Jewish Weekly Newspaper's headline was "Our motto: Stability and Calm. No reason to panic." Professor Horst Matzerath at the NS-Documentation-Center in Cologne. October 1992.

dow and looked out over her balcony and the drizzly autumn morning.

"We were *Drei-Tage-Juden,* (three day Jews), meaning we went to synagogue only on the High Holy-days, although we did have a tutor – Fräulein Kaplan – who came by the house every week to teach us Hebrew. In my private school in Grunewald, the three Jewish girls had a separate religion class while the non-Jewish girls studied Christianity." Hans and Paul went to school not far from home, and their father paid a rabbi who came by twice a week to teach them how to follow a prayer service and read Hebrew.

Throughout the 1920s, while the twins remained mischievous, their older sister concentrated on her studies, determined to make journalism her career. She began at Humboldt University. But suddenly the twenty-three years old student found all doors slammed shut. The year was 1935, the year the Nazis' Nuremburg Laws stripped Jews of their civil rights. "So that was that, and I took a job at the Jewish Culture Bund. I also became one of those who enjoyed the resurgence of Jewish life in Germany. And it was a real resurgence, because all our energies were now directed inward. Rabbis gave powerful sermons we all flocked to hear – men like Joachim Prinz and Max Nussbaum. There were wonderful concerts in the Oranienburger Strasse synagogue and you could go to lectures by some of the finest writers and scientists in the whole country. It was a second flowering of culture, but it was also like whistling in the graveyard – trying to keep your spirits up when you're afraid." And although every Jew in Germany saw what was happening on the streets, read the mood of the newspapers and heard the hatred on the radio, not everyone could, or would, make the move Elsie was soon to make.

She moved to the edge of her chair. "The Jewish boycotts – those were the first signals. Shop windows were smashed by Nazis, and they stood outside Jewish stores, lawyers' offices and doctors' practices and told people not to go in. We were lucky because my father's commanding officer from the war was a proper German officer. He liked my father very much and came and stood right outside the door so nothing would happen."

Soon after, Elsie married Eric Harding. He worked in his father's leather and fur business. During the Olympic Games of 1936, in a move to quiet protests from abroad, the Nazis gave Jews back their passports, which they had confiscated earlier. Eric Harding used his to make a business trip to London and told Elsie he would stop and visit his family in Holland on the way home. "After he left, I was seized with the thought that all our passports would be collected again after the Games," so without telling her husband, this fiesty young woman discussed matters with her parents, packed her things and took a train to Utrecht. "Eric found me sitting in our cousin's house and asked, 'why did you travel with so many suitcases?' And I said, 'I didn't travel. I left.' He stared at me, and I knew then, and I still know now: that man would never have left Germany."

Within two years, Elsie's brothers and parents made it out and the family re-established itself in London. The servants back in Berlin carefully wrapped up every piece of furniture, china and crystal and shipped it to England. Some of them came with the goods to help unpack, then tearfully left for home. At the age of sixty, Elsie's father taught himself English. Four years later he passed his examinations and set up a medical practice.

Elsie Harding stared down at the carpet, then back at me. "But look, there's one thing you must remember. Don't believe that German Jews didn't leave because they thought things would get better or because they trusted the Germans. They stayed for the simplest reason: because of their *parents*. Those sixty and over, they couldn't bring themselves to go. My parents were the exception. So many others, so very many others," she said quietly, "did not have our good fortune."

Elsie Harding squinted through the London mist. "See that apartment house over there through the trees? On the top floor, there's a man I used to take ballroom dancing with back in Germany. His family was not lucky. And further, just beyond Finchley Road, that's where Louis Hirschberg lives. He stayed around far longer than I did."

He did indeed and he wished he hadn't. A few weeks after I spoke with Elsie, on the ninth of November, the fifty-seventh anniversary of the Nazi pogrom called *Kristallnacht*, eighty-three years old Louis Hirschberg welcomed me in his modest flat in Green Croft Gardens. While his wife busied herself in the kitchen preparing tea, he placed a few Hebrew books on a table in his study and arranged them just so. A new student would be arriving shortly. For the past twenty years, Hirschy, as he is known, has guided nearly every Jewish boy in the Belsize Square synagogue congregation through bar mitzvah lessons, and has seen to it that on the big day, parents would smile, grandparents would grow misty, and Rabbi Rodney Mariner would breath a sigh of relief.

When Louis himself was of bar mitzvah age, he was living far from Green Croft Gardens, in the picturesque town of Küstrin, now in Poland. Straddling the Oder and Warta rivers, the town was dominated by a walled fortress. Here the young Friedrich the Great was imprisoned by his father in 1730. Napoleon stood on its walls after conquering Prussia in 1806.

At the turn of the century there were 25,000 Küstriners, of whom twenty-five were Jews. Louis Hirschberg, the second of two sons, was born in 1912 to Arthur and Henrietta. "We were completely integrated into our surroundings but also separate. On the one hand, the leader of the Jewish community was a city councilman and captain of the local hunting society. My father was the treasurer of the former Front Line Soldiers Association. But we knew and felt anti-Semitism. I remember being beaten up by one bully in school who was calling me 'dirty Jew,' and what I recall most was not the thrashing, but how the school director saw what was going on, turned and walked away."

Arthur Hirschberg had purchased a small clothing store from Josef Levy just after the First World War. It survived the steep devaluation and the wild inflation of the 1920s, and Arthur Hirschberg built it into the largest department store in town. By the early 1930s, it was quite a showplace,

Elsie Alexander Harding in her London flat. November 1995.

with seven handsome dress-windows fronting the main square. Arthur Hirschberg rode everywhere in a chauffeured limousine, which spirited him every few days to Berlin, where he watched after a second, smaller store in Köpenick, just outside Berlin.

Maintaining a Jewish life in Küstrin was not easy with such a small community, but everyone pitched in. There were weekend services led by Cantor Loewy, and a traveling rabbi was brought in for the holidays. Cantor Loewy was the community's schochet (kosher slaughterer). Louis and his brother Werner liked to tag along with him to the local stockyard where a few cows were kept separate for the community. During the festive holidays, Küstrin's Jews rented the main hall of the finest hotel. Louis's mother and her friends spent days cooking and baking kosher dishes. Children were ushered up on stage to sing the Hebrew songs they had practiced for weeks; the decorations hung and glittered from the rafters. A hired dance orchestra played late into the night and Jewish families from the villages nearby came in for the occasion.

Louis and his friends dutifully met their Hebrew teacher three afternoons each week, and as he finished high school the young man looked forward to entering university to study law. He never had that chance. At university, the students were turning so radical and rightist, "I simply couldn't stomach it," he said, shuddering. Soon there wouldn't even be the option of going to university. In 1936, Louis Hirschberg took a small flat in Berlin to make ends meet, he began teaching Latin and French privately. He had also started writing friends abroad about getting out of Germany.

Back in Küstrin, as his father watched, neighbors began to hang Nazi flags from their windows. After the boycotts, after a few rocks sailed through the store's windows, and as their Jewish neighbors studied maps and wrote letters and quietly slipped away, Arthur Hirschberg began to sell off his possessions. The store in Küstrin went first. The servants had to be let go. The car went as well. All the time the atmosphere in the town became more and more hostile. When almost everything they owned had been sold, the Hirschbergs boarded a train and headed for the anonymity of Berlin. They rented a small flat on Regensburg Strasse. "It was touching," Louis said. "With each sale, my father made a donation to Zionist organizations, which were training and funding young Germans to live in Palestine. He became a big believer in Zionism and spoke about it enthusiastically, but he himself could never make the step to leave. It just wasn't in him."

Louis kept writing friends hoping to find sponsorship outside Germany. His brother had already left for Australia and finally an old acquaintance agreed to help Louis in England. It was autumn 1938 and the documents were in the mail. But they had not arrived by the ninth of November. "I was on the *S-Bahn* riding through town – it was right about now, a bit before noon, on a day like this." He smiled slightly. "I saw smoke rising from the direction of the synagogue on Oranienburger Strasse and all I could think about was my parents. I hurried over to their flat but no one was there. Just as I turned to leave, there was a knock on the door.

"He was in a normal suit, he was a perfectly ordinary civil servant, and he had a piece of paper in his hand. He asked who I was and I told him. He looked at me. I looked at him. I was not on his list. Still, I had the right name, and he said quietly, 'Please come with me.' Then he added, almost gently, 'Do you have a winter coat? If you do, you'd better put it on.'"

Louis Hirschberg accompanied the man to the Wilmersdorf town hall. He and several other Jewish men were loaded onto a truck and taken to Gestapo headquarters. A caravan of lorries waited. "It was a sight: men in slippers, without shoes, without their glasses. Young men, middle-aged men, really old men. The SS were all around, and they flogged us into the trucks and sealed them. We drove off through the city, packed in like sardines. No light, completely dark, and it was sheer terror – not knowing where we were going. We drove on and on. We heard trams, so we were still in Berlin.

Then there were no more trams and the trucks went faster. "All of a sudden the lorries stopped and then came the screaming and the rifle butts and we were all driven out like cattle. We were in Sachsenhausen."

Some twelve thousand Jews, the great majority from Berlin, were brought to this camp over the next few days (another thirteen thousand were sent to Buchenwald and Dachau). They were imprisoned for a month or so, subjected to torture and treatment beyond imagining. Men were frogmarched until they collapsed, then kicked to death. Some were beaten with boards until their skulls cracked. Some were suffocated in air tight closets. Louis Hirschberg said, "Every day the SS beat and kicked us and sent us out on work patrol. We dug around a canal – backbreaking, murderous work. Old men collapsed and died; I carried the body of one back to the camp in my arms.

"There was an older man named Kohn. He was a mathematician and he had a goiter, and the guards enjoyed teasing him and tripping him up. The poor man kept falling, and they kept tripping him. Finally, after days of this, he could no longer get up and he lay there whimpering. One guard pointed to me and shouted, 'You there, pick him up by his earlobes!' I pretended I didn't hear and wondered what would happen next. But the guard lost interest. Dr. Kohn died."

One night Louis Hirschberg learned that his father was at Sachsenhausen. "I thought he had managed to evade all this, but he hadn't, and even though you weren't allowed to go from barracks to barracks, I crept around until I found him."

Arthur and Louis Hirschberg faced each other. Their heads were shaved. They wore prison garb. The father and son spoke in whispers for a few minutes. Then, between the patrolling SS guards, Louis crept, waited, hid, sweated and dashed back to his bed. Louis Hirschberg did not, could not, recall what they spoke about. He only said, "That was the last time I ever saw my father."

After three weeks the SS began releasing prisoners in batches of fifty per day. Louis Hirschberg was in one of the first groups. He collected his clothing and boarded an *S-Bahn* in Oranienburg. He rode into Berlin with a rabbi from Mecklenburg and the managing director of the Tietz department

Louis Hirschberg giving a bar mitzvah lesson in his London apartment. November 1995.

store. They sat together, saying nothing, staring at nothing. Once in town, they took three different trains. Louis took an *U-Bahn* to his mother's flat. While he was sitting there, a man walked up to him, drew back and slugged him. Mirroring the school director back in Küstrin a dozen years before, everyone on the train looked away, but by this time, Louis Hirschberg was hardly surprised. "I went straight to my mother's. My papers had come for England; I kissed her goodbye, I went home and changed and I left Germany."

Arthur Hirschberg was released from Sachsenhausen a few days later. He and his wife remained in Berlin until 1942, when they were collected and put on a train to the Riga ghetto. Just before they left, they wrote to Louis to say how glad they were he had escaped. In Riga, the great majority of the German Jews were shot by Germans serving with the SS. One of them was Küstrin's treasurer of the Former Front Line Soldiers Association of the Great War.

Ruth Meyer remembers moving into the family's stylish new home in Krefeld, Germany's leading textile center. The living room furniture was matched to the paneling and wainscoting on the walls. The kitchen gleamed with modern appliances. The bathroom had heated towel racks and a special stall with heat lamps for winter tanning. On the top floor, the children's bedrooms opened onto their own playroom and on the ground floor, a glass-walled winter garden looked out on a manicured lawn.

Ruth's father, Karl, was a shoe manufacturer's representative and had an office at home. In the evenings, Ruth's mother would sit in the living room reading Goethe, her favorite, or studied up on libretti of operas she was about to see. Servants cooked the meals and tended the house. Ruth and her sister Ilse attended the French lycée, and at home the girls' needs were looked after by a governess. But it was the chauffeur, Hans Aretz, Ruth liked best. Sitting in her kitchen in a Los Angeles suburb, she recalled the man fondly. "He was so handsome, so elegant. I used to sit with him just to talk. It was always *Herr* Aretz. And I was always *Fräulein* Meyer." Ruth blushed. "He even taught me how to smoke properly." After the Nuremberg Laws, the servants had to quit the family employ.

When the Nazis came to power, Karl Meyer refused to discuss leaving Germany. He still said no after the Nuremberg Laws and he was just as adamant after the boycotts. Even the morning after he heard that the massive Krefeld synagouge had been burnt on *Kristallnacht*, he tried to hold firm. "He said, 'I just heard on the radio that it's all over and there's nothing more to worry about. The Germans aren't going to let this sort of thing continue!' But just to be safe, he decided that we shouldn't stay at home that night."

That was when the Nazis came. First they found the water pipes in the higher floors and ripped them out. While water gurgled across the carpets and splashed down the stairs, they took hammers and axes and went to work. By the time they left at dawn, every piece of furniture, every piece of crystal, every cup and every window lay smashed, broken, destroyed. Water was still running down and through the walls and out into the street.

As the family picked through the ruins, and as Karl Meyer realized he had only been deluding himself, their former chauffeur Hans Aretz appeared. From that moment on, as the Meyers made plans to flee from Germany, Aretz and his wife clandestinely went wo work for them. First, Ruth and her sister were hustled off to the Aretz house to live. Then Herr Aretz carted the ruins of the

Meyer's house away. It took eleven truck loads. Frau Aretz began taking trips to Holland, and in her bags and around her neck were the silver and gold and jewelry Ruth's family had left. She went time and time again until she dared not put another Dutch visa in her passport.

Everyone in the family started phoning, telegraphing, writing letters and following leads on how to escape. In early summer, 1939, Ruth spotted an ad. "They were taking domestic servants in England. I applied through an agency and got the job. I lied about my age – I was seventeen, not nineteen – but I got the visa anyway. Everyone in the family was happy that I would be the first one out." Just before she was to leave, her father was arrested and thrown in prison. He had given some of the family silver to a friend to smuggle out of Germany and the friend had been caught and confessed. Horrified, the family was told the only way Karl Meyer would ever be allowed out is if he had an invitation and visa for another country. Now it would be up to his seventeen year old daughter to save him.

"I caught a train to Holland. At the border, I suddenly realized what trouble I was in. The German border police were looking through every single date and page of every document and my visa was predicated on my being nineteen." Alone in her compartment, Ruth was so terrified all she could think to do was feign illness and turned her head to the wall. The German officer slid open the door and stood before her, staring.

"That's when I heard, 'Raus!'" And she looked up to see that it was not the German yelling. It was a Dutch border guard behind him. The train had begun moving; the German was sent packing and Ruth slid down in the seat, relieved, safe, and in Holland.

In less than a week, the once-wealthy, now-impoverished French-speaking seventeen-year old showed up as a domestic on the doorstep of a farmhouse near Frinton-on-Sea. The family figured out rather quickly that this was no ordinary maid. She arrived with eleven matching suitcases.

Ruthie the rich girl was now Ruthie the char-

The Leo Baeck Institute in New York, a center for the historical study of German Jewish history. March 1995.

woman. In three days she proved such a disaster the owners of the house fired her. But from deep inside, she brought forth a strength she didn't know she had. She said she needed another chance. She promised she would improve. The family backed down.

The next day, she hurried to London and to Bloomsbury House, where a Jewish organization was helping process the tens of thousands of German-Jewish applications for visas, help, assistance. Ruth had to push her way through the crowd to a window, and she was told to fill out an application for her parents and that she would be contacted by post.

"Post?" Ruth said she needed help now. They told her to leave. "But I can't just leave," she stammered.

Ruth stumbled outside. She tried to think and all she could think to do was to sit down just where she was on the steps. After all the petitioners had turned in their forms and left, as rush-hour traffic and taxis and buses roared by at 5:00 PM, the staff was surprised to see a brooding teenage girl waiting for them on the steps. "What are you doing here child?"

Ruth looked at them and announced her simple plan for getting her father out of jail and her family out of Germany. "I am about to start screaming," she told them, "and I'm going to sit here and I'll keep screaming until the police take me away or people will wonder what you're doing or until you open that door and help me get my parents out of Germany!" Someone fumbled for a key.

Two weeks after that, in mid-August 1939, Karl and Marthe Meyer, along with Ilse boarded a train in Krefeld, then took a boat from Holland to England. Four days later, Germany invaded Poland, war was declared and the borders were sealed. For most of the Jews still left in Germany, so was their fate.

Aufbau office, New York. German Jews who settled in the United States founded the Aufbau, a German-language newspaper that had, in the 1940s, 60,000 subscribers. By 1995, it had less than 6,000. March 1995.

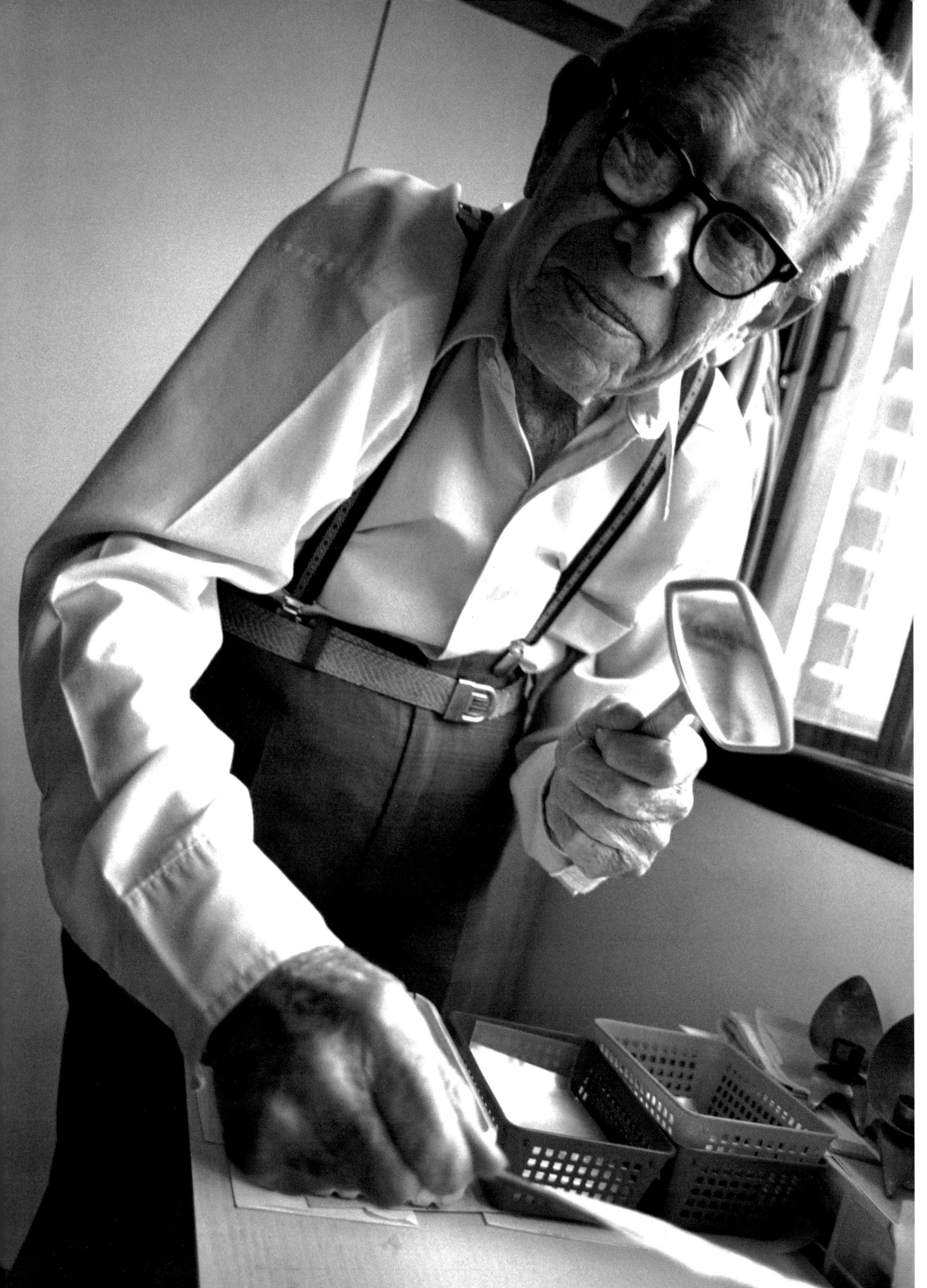

Jewish was our religion,
German is what we were

The Yekkes

No one is exactly sure of the origin of the Israeli slang word Yekke, which is what German Jews were called from the time they began arriving en masse in the 1930s.

Conventional wisdom has it that when the highly-educated and over-dressed men of Stuttgart and Dresden went to work in the fields, they often wore a suit jacket, or *Jacke* in German (J pronounced as Y). These bookish and fussy types were ill-prepared to be *kibbutzniks* and calling someone a Yekke was never complimentary.

Many Israelis then enjoyed seeing the mighty brought low and they worked to see it happen. After all, German Jewry had been less than welcoming to the Russian and Polish Jews who flocked to German cities in the decades before Hitler. *Too Jewish*, the German Jews of Düsseldorf and Hannover huffed as they looked down their noses at the poor *Ost-Juden* (eastern Jews). Now the shoe was on the other foot and attached to that foot were Polish and Russian Jews in positions of authority. It appears they used it often. But although their welcome may not have been overwhelming, some 50,000–60,000 Jews from Germany and Austria and other German-speaking communities fled to Pales-

Mordechai Virschubsky from Leipzig in his Tel Aviv office. January 1995

tine before and during the war and they stayed and tried to reconstruct the lives that had been torn apart back home in Europe. (One colorful example of how German Jewry looked down on others was manifested nakedly in a letter Hannah Arendt wrote to Karl Jaspers in 1961 while she was covering the Eichmann trial. "My first impression: On top, the judges, the best of German Jewry. Below them, the prosecuting attorneys, Galicians, but still Europeans. Everything is organized by a police force that gives me the creeps, speaks only Hebrew and looks Arabic... And outside the doors, the oriental mob, as if one were in Istanbul or some other half-Asiatic country.")

Mordechai Virschubsky was nine years old when his parents packed up and left Leipzig in 1939. What he remembered most was that for the three years before the family emigrated, his life was surrounded by rules: never go outside alone; do not play in the street. Worse, most of his friends had already gone and all this weighed heavily on him. "Suddenly we were living in Tel Aviv. Instead of being copped up inside cold and dreary Leipzig, now it was warm all the time and I was playing on the street day and night – and with other children. No one locked their doors. It was a totally free atmosphere and I adapted – like children do – with no problems at all."

Former Frankfurter Alfred Saenger, 91 years old, with his stamp collection in his room in the Siegfried Moses Old Age Home in Jerusalem. May 1995.

But what is easy for children is not so simple for adults. "My father fled Russia for Germany. He had suffered from pogroms under the Czar, and he completely rebuilt his life in Germany. Then at the age of forty-eight, he was forced to flee and start over yet again. It was too much.

"He opened a small shop on Ben Yehuda Street – number seven. He went from being a successful furrier in an elegant store to sitting in a tiny shop with bits of kitchenware and appliances. He was not successful. The difficulties piled up. It really hurt him, there was hostility to German Jews, and everything seemed to bear down on him. Not long ago, while looking through his papers, I found a copy of a letter he sent to the school authorities in Tel Aviv asking for a reduction in my tuition – and the tuition was barely a pittance! But he had next to nothing. Yet he never complained, and he took the comments about Yekkes inside. You

Gabriel Bach, who grew up in Berlin, is a supreme court judge in Israel and had been a prosecutor of Adolf Eichmann. May 1995.

see, he never overcame the shock of the move. He died when he was just fifty-eight, three weeks after the founding of the state of Israel." Later his son would go on to become the Speaker of the *Knesset*, Israel's parliament, and afterwards, vice mayor of Tel Aviv.

I left Virschubsky's office on an unseasonably mild June afternoon and wound my way on foot through the canyons of Bauhaus-era apartment buildings that crowd every inch of Tel Aviv. In one sharp-edged, narrow-windowed 1930s-era house, I knocked on the door of Hilda Hoffmann (née Kaufmann), president of the Association of former Frankfurt Jews. There are more than a dozen of these associations in Israel, although some of them are starting to peter out now. They arrange cultural meetings, card games, festivities, and they also maintain relations with their home towns – Hamburg, Stuttgart, Berlin and elsewhere. Some help arrange official visits, others try to encourage

school and church groups from their home towns to visit them in Israel. A few work with city-museums back in Germany to help create exhibitions that will tell of the world they lived in, the one they had before they were chased out of it. "Don't even think of including anything on Heinrich Heine!" a former Hamburg Jew barked to the mild-mannered Ortwin Pelc, a historian in charge of creating a Jewish department in the Museum of Hamburg History. Apparently he still could not forgive the nineteenth century poet for converting out of the religion.

These aging but ever-sprightly associations operate under the aegis of the *Irgun Olej Merkas Europa*, which bills itself as "the organization of former Central European Israelis." With what must be described as German (or *Yekke-ish*) efficiency, IOME runs old age homes, residences and seniors clubs. Through IOME, elderly German and Austrian and Bukovinin Jews have a place to go, someone to talk to, and someone who understands what it means to be a German Jew in the Promised Land. Hilda Hoffmann took over running the Frankfurt association in 1987 after her husband died. We chatted in her book-lined, primly furnished living room. Yellowed family portraits taken in another land stared out at us from their frames. As I looked around, I complimented her on this classic piece of German elegance. She smiled. "Well that's embarrassing," she said. "I bought every single piece of furniture in Israel."

One thing she did not have when she was growing up in Frankfurt was Zionism. Indeed, when Zionism – or, on the other hand, Nazism – was brought up at the dinner table, Albert Kaufmann, her father, laughed dismissively. Both these -isms would pass, the well-to-do shoe wholesaler told the family assuredly. Until, that is, he was picked up during the *Kristallnacht* pogrom and sent

Stein Books in Jerusalem has long been a repository for families of German Jews who wish to sell off the books their grandparents brought with them from Germany years before. October 1993.

to Buchenwald. He was imprisoned thirty-one days and he returned a shattered man. Not once did he speak of what happened inside the barbed-wire fences above Weimar, not to his daughter, not even to his wife. But the man who refused to consider leaving Germany suddenly couldn't get far enough away. "We took nothing. We just fled," she said, "and we had to be smuggled out of Germany to Holland on New Year's Eve, 1939. We went across the border in a horse-drawn wagon, buried underneath the driver.

"Actually, my mother, Selma, wanted to stay in Holland. It was Europe; it wasn't so different than what we had known. But not my father. Once he had made the move to leave Frankfurt, Holland was out of the question. It was too close to Germany and we took one of the first ships bound for Palestine."

Hilda was sixteen years old when the family arrived. "The Tel Aviv I came to was a thin band stretched along Ben Yehuda Street. You knew everyone. You spoke German. And life was so different then. We would walk down to the sea, pick oranges and sit on the beach in the evenings, eating and talking. We listened to classical music on little phonographs and everyone just walked in

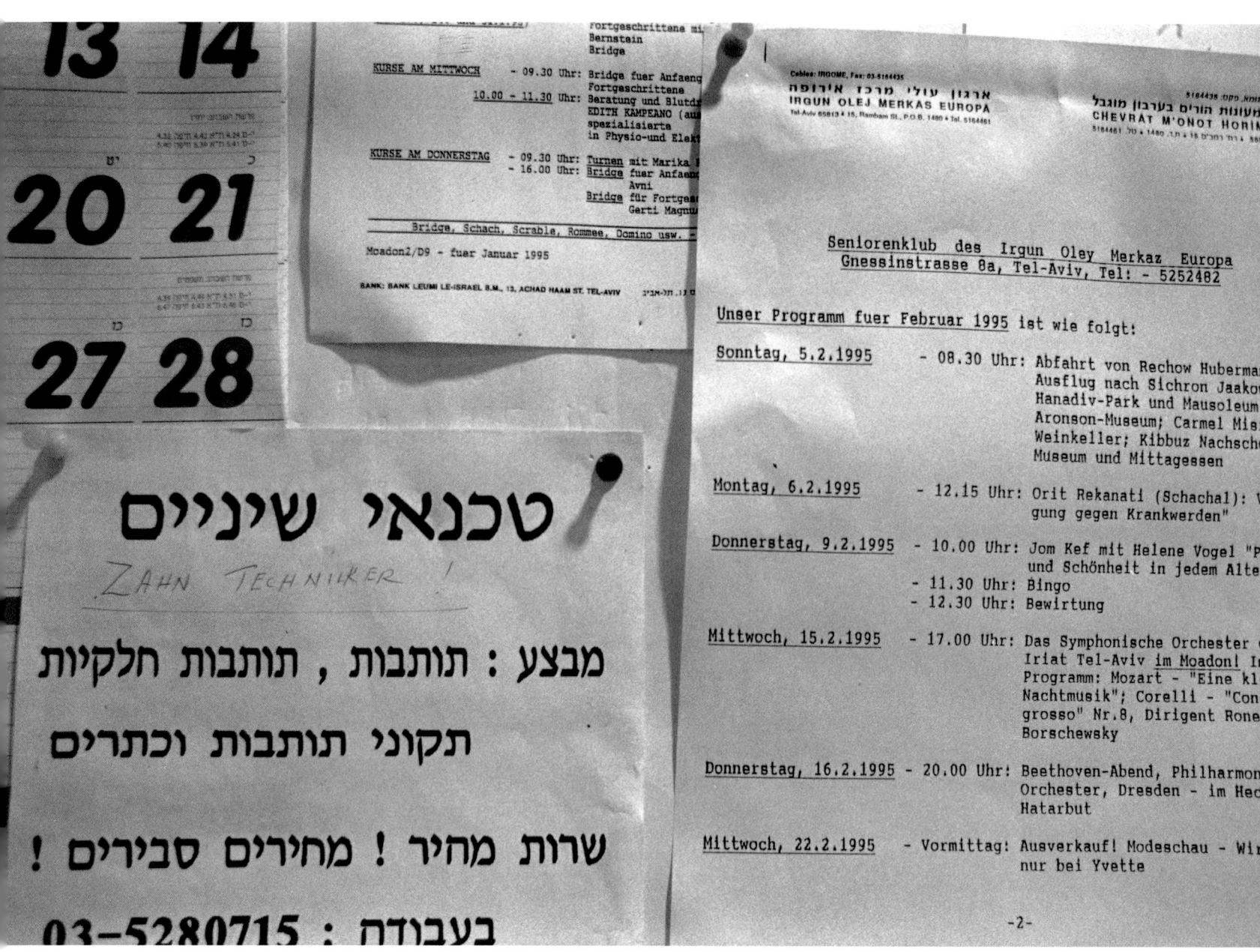

Bulletin board in a social center for German Jews. Tel Aviv. January 1995.

and out of everyone else's apartments. Obviously we were poor – a lot poorer than we were in Frankfurt. But these are not problems for the young. I remember going to the symphony with my parents. We'd buy two tickets and then we'd trade-off. One of us would sit through the entire performance, but the other two would trade during the intermission. Then we'd all walk home together talking of the music. That's how much we loved culture." She paused. "And that's how poor we were."

Like Mordechai Virshubsky's father, Albert Kaufmann faced overwhelming odds. For him they would prove insurmountable. "He started a small shoe factory and he failed at it. You would never hear him complain – complaining was not the style of this whole generation – but it must have been awful. Life was so hard here for German Jews of their generation, and my father had little choice. In the early 1950s, he and my mother announced they were moving back to Frankfurt. Jewish restitution was possible then and he had claims to make. And it was just as hard for him there – but of course in a completely different way. Again, he took it stoically, but not long after he arrived, he took sick and died. My mother died afterwards and I thought then that the only reason I would ever return to Germany would be to visit their graves."

The claims Albert Kaufmann made became possible because of the Luxembourg Agreements. As early as 1945, leaders of the *Yishuv,* Israel's de-facto government under British rule, submitted a request to the Allied Powers asking for reparations against post-war Germany. And while it is not the task of this book to discuss the process and procedures that took place in 1951 and 1952 (see bibliography), West Germany's first chancellor, Konrad Adenauer, a conservative man of deep Roman Catholic belief, spearheaded his government's path to the negotiating table. Adenauer's own religious conviction convinced him that to make such reparations was the only honorable thing to do, even though the move went against the overwhelming opinion of the German people.

Not that Israelis welcomed the idea of German restitution, either. When it was announced that in early January 1952, the *Knesset* would discuss whether or not to open these negotiations, a young and demagogic Menachim Begin led a charge against the government building. Thousands shouted from outside, many broke windows and the building had to be cordoned off with barbed wire and guards. Begin screamed, "What price are we going to get for grandpa and grandma?" Prime Minister David Ben Gurion answered back, "Let not the murderers of our people be also their inheritors!" (Tom Segev, The Seventh Million, New York 1992)

The first meeting between German and Israeli negotiators was held in the Hague in March 1952. The Israelis claimed one and a half billion dollars from Germany, of which two-thirds was demanded from West Germany. English was used at the initial meeting, not German. No one shook hands. For the first time in modern history, however, a victimized ethnic group sat down to bargain with the perpetrators of its victimization for compensation.

Discussions did not always go smoothly. On one occasion the Israeli delegation walked out. At another point, two German negotiators quit and publicly distanced themselves from their state's position. But in September 1952, formal agreements were signed in the Luxembourg City Hall. Again, hands were not shaken in public. No one would go so far as to applaud the decision. And the Israelis wrote into the contract that acceptance meant neither "recognition nor conciliation." And it was not until more than a decade later, in 1965, that Israel and Germany established formal diplomatic relations. (The Seventh Million, Tom Segev, New York 1992)

Between 1952 and 1966, Germany provided Israel three quarters of a billion dollars in goods: metals, oil, industrial and chemical products. This accounted for between twelve and fourteen percent of Israel's imports during that critical time of nation-building. The agreements also allowed families who lost property, languished in concentration camps or had family members killed make claims against the West Geran state. (The East Germans steadfastly refused to discuss the matter). Over one thousand lawyers in Israel filed tens of thousands of claims. Many claimants filed from their homes in Israel. (West German Reparations to Israel, Nicholas Balabkins, New Jersey 1971) Others, like Hilda Hoffmann's parents, returned home to do so.

Germany was paying Israel, but in Israel, German Jews continued to suffer unparalleled discrimination. "If you spoke German on the bus, someone would yell – *Yekke putz!*" said Hilda Hoffmann. "They told jokes about the slow and plodding Yekkes." Virschubsky recalls that an uncle of his came to Jerusalem from Germany to teach at the university and found his colleagues so hostile that he simply packed up and moved to Princeton.

In time, however, the edges wore down, the hostility became more muted, and as the years passed it was no longer even an issue. More to the point, German Jews made important contributions to Israeli society in nearly every field. "Okay, true enough, the German Jews – the Yekkes – never had the *chutzpah* of the Russian and Polish Jews," said Virschubsky. "They were born to be polite, and in Israel, they remained – and still remain – polite." He drummed his desk then stabbed the air with a finger. "But the legal machinery of the state and the posts that have to do with financial accountability, these were the realms of the Yekkes, because in these fields you need someone honest, disciplined and straight."

"But to initiate?" He shook his head. "It took a Polish Jew to start the symphony orchestra. But it was the Germans who filled the audience and made up God knows how many of the players."

Supreme court judges, editors of respected newspapers, publishers, scientists – many were German Jews and they contributed much to the vitality of the newborn state. Still, Israeli society tended to marginalize their achievements and had difficulty in recognizing their worth. Handling Holocaust survivors was difficult enough. But many Israelis spent years condemning German Jews for letting what Israelis saw as a slavish attachment to the Fatherland blind German Jewry to its evil. Zionism, like most -*isms*, is short on tolerance for those who traduce its most sacred tenants.

In the years since the War, there has been much rewriting of history. German Jews have tried hard, with books and exhibitions, to prove they had always been ardent Zionists, although the vast majority were not. And Israelis have started coming around to seeing the Yekkes *not* as slow and plodding, but instead as careful and meticulous.

Now being called a *Yekke* is not so negative. I recall fetching a teenager from his Jerusalem high school one afternoon and the directress of the school had me fill out papers and forms for stating my responsibility. I chided her a little and asked, "Are you a *Yekke*?" She laughed. "No I'm not, unfortunately, and I wish we had learned more from them!" She thought for a minute. "Now that we really need them, now that we're more willing to listen, I'm afraid it's too late."

By the 1990s, the German Jews who had fled to Palestine in the 1930s were either dead or elderly. As they grew older, as memory faded, as illnesses and strokes came, they moved to old age homes. Not far from Jerusalem's colonial-period train station is the Siegfried Moses Home, named for Israel's first State Controller – a German Jew. Here, of the one hundred-ten residents, sixty-five percent speak German. Twenty years ago, the percentage was higher: one hundred percent.

The residents of the Moses Home hail from Czernowitz, Vienna, Berlin, Innsbruck, Zagreb – a virtual address book of Central Europe. Ninety-year-old Frau Sonnenblum is from Graz. "I saw Kaiser Franz Josef ride by when I was young," she said as she drifted slowly past in her wheelchair.

Recapturing Memory. Stephen Spielberg's Survivers of the Shoah Visual History Foundation has been video-interviewing Holocaust survivors throughout Israel, Europe and the rest of the world so that a permanent record of survivors testimonies will be permanently archived. Los Angeles, November 1995.

Page 38/40
Adi Ithion playing Marlene Dietrich in a Tel Aviv theater. October 1993.

40

One-hundred-one-year-old Trude Frankel is from Mannheim. "My father brought wine to the captain of the very first Zeppelin," she said, her eyes twinkling. "My father," she sighed as she shook her head, "he was *meschugge* for the Kaiser."

Alfred Saenger, 91 years old, and from Frankfurt, collects stamps from around the world, sells them to shops, then uses the proceeds to give to the home where his mentally-handicapped daughter lives. "And you know something interesting? A young man, Dieter, from Munich, comes by to visit me every week. He cares for my daughter, he's a volunteer there, but I think he likes to speak a little German sometimes, so he visits me and we just chat." He cocked his head slightly and looked at me. *"Können Sie Deutsch sprechen?"*

"Natürlich," I replied.

"Wunderbar," he said, and moving his chair closer to mine, he began, *"Als ich ein junger Mann in Frankfurt war…"*

Rifka Gerling ("but I was born Else") is the librarian at the home and has lived here eight years. Her ailing husband, an attorney who worked for decades with Siegfried Moses himself, is also in the home. Her parents were killed during the Holocaust. Her children have moved away from Israel. Sitting with her in the library, she studied a list of overdue books. There were no customers, and at noon she closed up shop. "I've been a Pole, a German, a Palestiner and an Israeli," she said, turning to me. "That's enough for one life, and there are many, many stories to tell." She looked over at the bookshelves, as if she was measuring up the stories they contained. She watched a couple outside in the hallway slowly making their way toward the dining hall. "Nearly everyone in this home has lived through one kind of hell or another – some have lived through several." Then she stood up and locked the library door. Rifka Gerling moved on, and stopped for a moment to chat in German with a doctor from Munich. She made her way past the lounge where people were reading *Stern* and *Der Spiegel* and paused outside the dining room to read the day's menu, written in both Hebrew and German. *"Tafelspitz!"* she said. Smiling, she turned to me. "It's quite fine. I recommend it."

Jewish was our religion,
German is what we were

Home Again

Sometimes in German high schools, but not often, instead of the usual guest speaker – a doctor who works in Africa, for instance, or an environmentalist who saves trees – they get a Jew. Someone old, someone born in Germany, right in their home town. And when an actual person sits before a room full of teenagers – not some Holocaust documentary film flickering away on a two dimensional screen – it can make them sit up, especially when the guest says in clear, distinct Geman, "I was just your age when I was thrown out of my school, when my Christian friends all turned away from me, and some of my Jewish girlfriends went to their deaths in the gas chambers of Auschwitz." You can almost see the sixteen and seventeen year olds calculate. You are as old as my grandmother. My grandmother was alive then, the same age as your girlfriends. And she doesn't speak about the past except to say how tough the rationing was.

Then hands go up; questions blurt out; dialogue begins.

How do these German Jews, who escaped from or lived through the Nazi period, relate to the land of their birth? Each has had a radically different experience, and those experiences dictate their feelings today: some want nothing at all to do with Germany or the people in it. Others seem compelled to visit, and keep visiting.

During World War Two, while their sister Elsie Harding was tending her firstborn in London, Hans

Leo Baeck Old Age Home, London. Most German Jews never returned home. Of the 50,000 who came to England before the war, the majority remained. February 1993.

and Paul Alexander enlisted in the British Army. "It was quite exciting," Hans said with an ironic twitch of his eyebrows. "They let us fill sandbags." Because the brothers came from Germany, they were considered enemy aliens and kept behind in Britain to do manual labor for most of the war. It was only in 1945 that they were shipped over to the Continent.

"I was sent to a town called Belsen," Hans Alexander said as he sat on a sofa next to his elegantly-dressed wife Ann in their London flat. "We arrived eight days after liberation and for a while, all we could do was clean up the camp." He stopped, then repeated the words, "clean up." He shook his head, dissatisfied at how poorly the words described what he had seen. "The inmates – they were skeletons in pyjamas – they would shuffle up to you and beg for food, and if you were kind and stupid, you gave them something, like chocolate, which made them so sick some of them died. Our doctors forced us to stop giving them our rations, but what could you say when someone like that was begging?

"We also made the local population – you know, the ones who 'didn't know a thing' – we brought them in to do a lot of the work. And while I was there, I was told that my job was changing. I was to begin looking for Nazis."

The British Army ordered Hans Alexander and other German-speaking soldiers to seek out high ranking Nazis and gather evidence against them for trials. For the next twelve months, Hans Alexander went into homes, offices and churches. He interviewed the young, the elderly and those in between. He took notes, cross-referenced, kept asking. After the first hundred interviewees he lost count. And still he kept going. When the files were well-documented enough, there came arrests, interrogations and prison.

"Naturally, no one knew anything, not about Nazis, not about Jews." He smiled a wry, bitter smile. "In Fallingbostel the mayor told me they never had a Jew there. I let it go and said nothing and started to drive out of town. But just fronting the highway was a Jewish cemetery. I turned the car around and threw the mayor in jail for a while. At least he should be moderately clever when telling such bald-faced lies.

"In all the hundreds of interviews I made, I met a total of three Nazis – not more. One was the police chief of Hamburg, another was a naval officer, and the third, well that was Rudolf Hoess, the commandant of Auschwitz."

Rudolf Hoess had been one of the earliest Nazis and made his career in the concentration camp system starting in Dachau in 1933. As an SS captain he was transferred to Sachsenhausen in 1938. Later, he moved his wife and five children into the camp grounds at Auschwitz, which had not yet become the factory of death it would later be infamous for. Rudolf Hoess went to work each morning to find ways of massacring the most number of Jews in the most efficient manner possible. When he wrote his memoirs, *"Kommandant in Auschwitz,"* in a Polish prison shortly before being hung in 1947, he seemed proud of the fact that he was the first to use *Zyklon B* gas during the war. He also regretted that in 1943 he was transferred from Auschwitz to a desk job near Sachsenhausen. He must have been pleased, then, to return in the summer of 1944. In the last great Nazi push for Jewish extermination, Adolf Eichmann relocated to Budapest and deported the great majority of Hungarian Jews to Poland. His partner became the ever-efficient Hoess, and between June and August, more than a half million Hungarian Jews were gassed.

Yet Hoess, in his memoirs, insisted, "I am completely normal. Even while I was carrying out the task of extermination I lived a normal life and so on." And being a military man, he wrote that he was treated fairly by his Polish captors. It was only the arrest that was not to his liking and he said he was treated "cruelly." That arrest was made by Hans Alexander.

"We found Frau Hoess living in Heide along with some of her children," Alexander recalled. "They told us nothing, of course, so we left. So we put a tail on everyone. Working in plain clothes, we followed Frau Hoess and after a while she led us directly to her husband. He was in a farmhouse around five kilometers from the Danish border, ready to flee. We approached the farmhouse at night, surrounded it and I went to the door. Hoess himself answered it. He was wearing pyjamas and as soon as the door cracked my pistol went straight down his throat – we'd been warned they kept poison pellets in their mouths. You know this is how we lost Himmler after he was captured. Bit down on a poison capsule and died surrounded by British soldiers."

"Naturally he said he wasn't Hoess and he had enough false ID to prove it. He even had his SS blood-type tattoo removed from under his arm. He kept insisting and I kept telling him he was lying. Suddenly I looked down and noticed his wedding ring. 'Give it to me,' I said. 'Oh I can't, he said. 'It's been stuck for years.' 'No problem', I said, 'I'll just cut your finger off and we'll be able to look that way.' I sent for a kitchen knife and by the time it arrived, the ring was off. He just sat there glaring at me. Inside was his and his wife's names. I thanked him, flipped the ring into my pocket and stood up. The room was filled with Jews – boys from Germany who bad been chased out of the country, and some of whom who had lost their parents in Auschwitz. I walked to the door and said, 'I want Hoess in my car in ten minutes. No bruises.' I turned and left."

Hans Alexander remained with the British Army in Germany until late 1946. During that time he continued his interviews, sought the guilty, dismissed the innocent, and tried to understand the difference between the two. After he had built up a handful of cases against murderers and torturers of every description, he had the agonizing duty of trying to convince the victims of these grotesque, degrading crimes to stay and testify. Some of these victims were still recovering in Belsen's hospital. Some fell apart just trying to remember. Others simply couldn't bring themselves to sit in court and face those who had injected poison into children just to time how long it took them to writhe their way to death, or those who had poured icy water on the bare chests of men to see how long it would take to bring about heart attacks. Horror after horror after horror. "The number of murderers I had to let go sickened me," Alexander muttered, shaking his head. "They played us for fools. The Russians were more effective, you see. When they heard such stories, they found the accused, pulled out a pistol and shot them. We couldn't do that. We didn't do that."

It was quiet in the room. Hans Alexander stood up. He had rarely talked of this part of his past and it was clear he'd reached an end point for the day. Outside, it had turned dark, and from this seventh floor apartment, the lights of London winked and glittered all around us. "And now," he said, "That's enough. It's time for a drink." He poured two glasses of scotch; we raised our glasses and said *"la Chaim."* After a minute or two, he looked as if he wanted to say

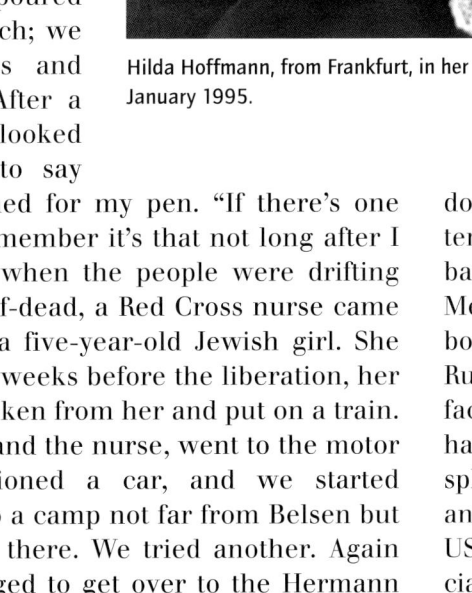

Hilda Hoffmann, from Frankfurt, in her Tel Aviv apartment. January 1995.

something. I reached for my pen. "If there's one thing I'll always remember it's that not long after I arrived at Belsen, when the people were drifting around like the half-dead, a Red Cross nurse came up to me holding a five-year-old Jewish girl. She said that just a few weeks before the liberation, her mother had been taken from her and put on a train. So I took the child and the nurse, went to the motor pool and requisitioned a car, and we started driving. We went to a camp not far from Belsen but her mother wasn't there. We tried another. Again no luck. We managed to get over to the Hermann Göring Works, the Volkswagen factory in Wolfsburg. And there I took the loudspeaker and I called out the mother's name." A cry went up from the factory yard and a woman tore her way through the crowd toward the office, toward the child inside. You know, that was the only worthwhile thing –" and his voice cracked, "the *only* worthwhile thing I

did in six and a half years." In the decades that followed, Hans became a merchant banker and Paul went to work in the building industry. Between them they have five children, twelve grandchildren and two greatgrandchildren.

"And would I go to Germany to speak with school children?" Hans Alexander said. He smiled indulgently. "Look. I don't have any trouble with young Germans. Naturally, I look at the older generation and I want nothing to do with them. But you can't look at a fifteen year old or even a forty-five year old German and hold this against them. But no, I wouldn't talk to school children because children should not be taught to hate. And hate is what I've got."

Ruth Meyer and her family left England in 1940 on United States visas and family connections helped secure them a small apartment in downtown Chicago. This once-rich family no longer had maids, drivers and fine clothes. Her father went to work selling Fuller brushes door to door; he dragged his sample cases up and down tenement steps, winter and summer. Just as he had back in his elegant townhouse in Krefeld, Carl Meyer spent his evenings going over his account books. Only now there wasn't much to go over. Ruth's mother's first job was in a steam-filled jam factory and she came home in the evenings exhausted, her hands and arms stained and splotched. College was no longer an option for Ruth and she studied to become a beautician. She met a US Army captain, Eddie Elcott, at a Jewish USO social in 1942. The young man looked smashing in uniform, he was a terrific dancer and a few weeks later he asked Ruth to marry him. Ruth said yes. Eddie was studying then at Northwestern University and upon graduation, the newlyweds packed up and moved, with millions of other Americans to California. While he worked at Lockheed and later taught political science in high school and at a community college, Ruth worked as a hairdresser. They had three sons, and in the mid 1950s, after the death of Ruth's father, her mother came to live with them. She never spoke of the past and she and her daughter did not converse in German. This was an American family. Germany and everything in it was behind them, except the nightmares Ruth had nearly every night. Eddie would calm her, talk with her, and then they'd go back to sleep.

One day Ruth received a call at work. There was an exchange student coming to Los Angeles and she needed a place to stay. "Not a problem", Ruth said. "We're on the list." But she heard something in the woman's voice. No other family would take the girl. "Why", Ruth asked. "Because she's German." "Well I can't either" snapped Ruth and she hung up quickly. But that didn't make her feel any better. The next morning, Ruth phoned back. "Send the child to me", she said. And around the dinner table the following night, a perky seventeen-year old blonde girl sat across the table from Ruth and her mother and the rest of the family. With three teenage boys at the table, there was hardly a lack of conversation, but one thing was nagging at the student. She turned to Marthe Meyer and said, "I hear you have a German accent."

The old woman looked up and said quietly, "That's the only thing the Nazis didn't take away from me." There was silence around the table for a moment; it was the first time Ruth had ever heard her mother refer to the past before a stranger. The boys salvaged the conversation and moved it on.

The German girl stayed with Ruth and her family for a couple of weeks, then left. Her stay did nothing to change Ruth's feelings, or stop those nightmares. It took another German teenager to do that.

One day in 1967, just before Ruth and her sons were leaving to spend six months in Israel, Eddie presented her with a letter from a high school student in Krefeld. It was a request from a girl for Ruth to make an interview on tape. Somehow, the girl had tracked Ruth down; she wrote that she was sorry about what happened in the past and she wanted to know about Ruth's childhood. She closed the letter by wishing Ruth a merry Christmas.

"At first I didn't want to have anything to do with it, but I answered it. I said that naturally, it was not her fault what happened, but in a way, she must bear the guilt of her parents just as my children bear my own pain. I sent it off and left for Israel."

The tape made its way from the high school to the local Krefeld newspaper, where the editors ran an uncut transcript. The morning it appeared, in home after home in Krefeld, telephones rang. Krefeld women called each other to speak about little Ruthie Meyer, Ruthie they went to the *Lycee* with, Ruthie who they went to the movies with, Ruthie, their friend. Or was it ex-friend? Does she hate them now? Had she always? The classmates met soon after at the home of Dorle Englender and sitting around her dining room table, they wrote a letter and mailed it to California.

A few months later, Eddie Elcott arrived in Israel to join his family. Ruth and he had planned to pick up a Volkswagen they had ordered in Austria, then drive throughout Europe, avoiding Germany at Ruth's request. We've changed our plans, Eddie told her. You're going back to school.

Ruth's first reaction was completely negative. She felt that she could simply not cross the German border. The trauma of her leaving Germany decades ago, the German border policeman looming above her was still too horrid to contemplate. She was nearly panicked.

"But this was an easy problem to fix," Eddie recalled nearly thirty years later. "Dorle Englender met us in Salzburg, in Austria, and in less than a minute Ruth and she were yakking non-stop. Decades of news began flooding out of these two, and it was everything I could do to shove them in the backseat of the little Beetle. I drove off, sailing right through the border and into Bavaria before either of them had any idea we'd slipped into Germany. They didn't stop to ask where we were until we were halfway to Munich."

Ruth smiled an embarrassed smile and looked fondly at her husband.

The threesome drove north toward Krefeld and a few days later Ruth entered the house of one of her schoolmates. Eighteen of the twenty-one girls

Jerusalem and Freiburg high school students spending an afternoon drawing and painting and tracing each other during an exchange program at the Denmark school in Jerusalem. October 1993.

in her class were there. The air was electric. Everyone was apprehensive. Ruth walked up to each one and told them their names. Now would the accusations start? they wondered. Ruth recalled, "I held back at first. I listened to their stories. They had lost a child after the war to an anti-tank mine. Lotte's husband had died because of wounds. Rose Marie, her sister also stepped on a landmine. Others were killed in the carpet bombing during the war."

Then Ruth began her own story, about that train ride, scrubbing farm house-floors, trying to get her parents out, their new life in Chicago. What was ironic was that Ruth was the only person in the room who had not lost an immediate family member due to the war. Indeed, Ruth had ten grandchildren. Her classmates didn't have that many between them. The old classmates talked long and emotionally that night. Ruth Elcott never had another nightmare.

Ruth stayed in Krefeld several weeks. Her relationships with old friends deepened and she made new friends as well. After that, Eddie and she visited Krefeld whenever they were vacationing in Europe. In 1988, two new friends, Renata and Helmuth Starck, activists in the Protestant church, offered to bring Ruth back to Krefeld for an official visit. Ruth insisted that if she accepted the invitation she would do so only if she could talk to school children, and read to them the diaries she kept when she was their age.

The Starcks jumped at the opportunity and spread the word to area schools. Fifteen principals asked Ruth to come and in order to prepare for Ruth's visit, teachers began working with their students so they could better learn of Jewish history, the Holocaust, the Jews of Krefeld. They made class projects on concentration camps, there were tables and graphs that covered whole walls that showed the route of surviving Krefeld Jews and those who perished. Teenagers were flocking to the library, the city archives. They were phoning up and researching in the Nazi archive centers in Düsseldorf and Cologne. They were asking permission to sit in on synagogue services in Cologne.

Israeli soldiers at Israel's Holocaust Memorial, Yad Vashem. October 1993.

Ruth arrived, and in fifteen schools in ten days, she sat in more classrooms than she could count, opened her dogeared little diary, and from inside that book, a frightened and confused sixteen year old Krefeld girl reached across half a century to tell other Krefeld teenagers what it was like to be spit on in the streets, chased off park benches, watch your best friends turn away from you, step over the rubble and litter and ruin of your hause, watch your mother sob, and flee on a train for your very life. Some kids openly wept. Others looked down and avoided Ruth's eyes. Few indeed left unaffected.

One evening, parents attended a social event for Ruth in one of the high schools and Ruth spoke with the parents just as she had with their children. The diary came out, she read to a silent chamber, and after she spoke, one after another of these forty-something adults stood up and said, we are the lost generation. It was our parents who refused to ever speak of the war, the Holocaust, and it was our teachers who never taught us a thing. Some men and women sat and cried. Some railed at their past, their country, their parents. And Ruth Meyer Elcott, the quiet catalyst, sat and listened.

Ruth Elcott was hardly the only Jew to return to Germany or even Krefeld for that matter. Throughout the country, cities and towns invited former Jewish residents back for official visits. Berlin was one of the first cities to sponsor such trips and by 1995, 40,000 Berlin Jews and their family members had been brought to the city to meet with officials, look for their old addresses and sometimes, to talk with students. Some leave more at ease with the present. Some leave optimistic for the future. Some leave more at ease with the past. And some leave more troubled and upset than when they came. But still the invitations go out, and still the Jews return.

In Tel Aviv, Hilda Kaufmann, who had fled from Frankfurt to Israel with her parents, married Hans Hoffmann. His father had been the chief rabbi of Frankfurt and Hans had fled Germany for Switzerland in 1933. Hans Hoffmann had business dealings in Frankfurt after the war, and he felt it was his responsibility, right from the beginning, to begin building bridges between Israel and Germany. He always thought about the youth and he welcomed

the chance to speak with school children, church youth groups. "'If we don't go and speak to German school children, who will?' he asked me very early on", Hilda Hoffmann said. "In one way, I knew he was right. After all, if my own father never once spoke of what happened to him during his thirty-one days in Buchenwald, it was clear Germans that age weren't going to sit around and talk about it. But I had my problems with this. I just didn't want to have anything to do with it. As I said, for me Frankfurt was where I went to visit graves, not talk to Germans.

"But throughout the 1960s, he never relented, and in time, I joined my husband in visiting schools. It was hard at first, but in time, I got used to it. And now I do it quite a bit." She seemed to draw herself up a bit when she said, "Tel Aviv is a sister city with Frankfurt, and from the 1960s on, we have been arranging exchanges of high schoolers each year. A hundred here, a hundred there, and after my husband founded the Association of former Frankfurt Jews, we Frankfurt Jews go back to visit, to see, to talk with children."

The work was never easy, but Hans Hoffmann forged ahead. He and his wife even extended an invitation to Germany's first ambassador to Israel to join them for a Passover seder in 1965. "It was not what I'd call a normal visit," said Hilda Hoffmann. "There was so much hostility toward the ambassador when he first arrived that the police had to block off the entire street when he came here that night."

Hans Hoffmann died in the 1980s and his wife has carried on in his place. He did not live to see German youths standing and dancing and laughing on the Berlin Wall. He did not live to see the country reunified. He also did not live to see tens of thousands of German students marching through the streets protesting against the Gulf War, as they loudly proclaimed that the Allies should stop bombing Iraq, even while Saddam Hussein's scud missiles tore into apartment houses in Tel Aviv.

True enough, there were protests throughout Europe against the American-led war against the Iraqis, but the sight of Germans marching against the war, the attitudes against it by many Germans who decried the use of force and violence, sent Jewish-German-Israeli friendship societies into nosedives. Some relationships crashed completely and never recovered. As she thought about those dark days in 1991, Hilda Hoffmann wrung her hands. "It was a terrible shock. Now, you must know that we got many, many letters from people – strangers we had never met – all from Frankfurt – offering to take our children and grandchildren. But the images on television, German politicians actually saying the Israelis brought this on themselves, the student on television who said he wanted to go to Iraq and help Saddam Hussein – oh how this hurt." While Israel was being attacked and while sympathy for the Jewish state poured out of the United States, Britain, Canada and elsewhere, German housewives were panic-buying in grocery stores, white sheets were hung out of apartment house windows and students carted around signs reading "I'm afraid." As the old World War Two Allies delivered bombs on an enemy state, citizens of the previous enemy state went into near hysterics. In Amsterdam, Dutch students marched for Israel. Across the border, German students were offering to go to Iraq. There were marchers in support of the war in Germany and donations from non-Jewish Germans to Israeli charities jumped that year to fifteen percent of gross proceeds from the usual three to five percent. Yet the mood among most left-of-center Germans seemed to be rather anti-American, and by extension, anti-Israeli.

"I was sick, I was furious, but most of all, furious with myself that I was so trusting, that I believed in them. Yes, yes there were discussions and many old friends were supportive. But nowhere else was there such a mood, such a large percentage of people so frightened and panicked by the war as in Germany, so ready to understand and even side with Saddam Hussein. And while it was clear it was anti-American oriented, what upset me most was the young people who were so vocal, the ones I had been speaking to for so long, so often." She was quiet for a moment. Then Hilda Hoffmann sighed and her hands clamped down on the arms of her chair. I asked how the Gulf War affected her own work, her own bridge building.

"I decided to begin again," she said firmly. "To work even harder. Yes, okay, sometimes the news is bad – but that's what news is – bad. It has taken some time, but now we've shaken off even this black period. We go on. We have to. Because after we're gone, those of my generation, there will be no witnesses left, no German Jews who can sit with a class of German youngsters and talk about what we went through – *in their language.*"

As I stood up to leave, Hilda Hoffmann said, "You know, until recently, I have rarely spoken of my past. It was always easier for me to send journalists to other people, other friends who were more willing to speak. I still don't do it much. You can't imagine how hard it is. Now I save my energies for those times I go into Frankfurt schools. That's where they're needed most."

Past Masters

Sometimes the irony stings: the bearded man in neatly pressed rabbinical robes raised his kiddish cup and recited the prayer over the wine as I clicked the shutter. Only he was no rabbi, rather an actor in a Berlin production of *Fiddler on the Roof*. In Cologne, I visited a family so strictly orthodox it reminded me of my grandparents' home. Only my Jewish grandparents were different from this cheerful young couple's grandparents – mine, unlike theirs, had not been in the Waffen SS.

Germans on Jews, Germans become Jews. Things Jewish could hardly be more popular in this country of eighty million Germans where fewer than sixty thousand Jews currently live. Klezmer bands and theater productions of Shalom Aleichem stories play to packed houses. More German, non-Jewish, high school students visit Israel each year than their American *Jewish* counterparts. Scores of exhibitions on Jewish history and memorials commemorating the Holocaust open annually. And grandchildren of Nazis go abroad to work in Israeli hospitals, study Hebrew and, on occasion, feel the need to convert.

This evolution from state-sponsored anti-Semitism to grass roots philo-Semitism took the best part of the past half century and the results are still patchy. Its sometimes dark twists and embarrassing turns reveal the tortured task of a nation trying, and sometimes failing badly, to come to grips with a uniquely awful past.

In the first years after the Second World War, since Nazism was a home-grown product, it was

Gottfried Strehle, a German actor in Fiddler on the Roof, in Berlin's Metropol Theater. May 1993.

well-nigh impossible to root out all believers from positions of authority. It is not at all clear that every village, town and city tried to do so. Nearly one in eight of the adult population belonged to the Nazi and related parties. Many Nazi judges, school teachers, doctors remained at their posts. Karl Jaspers wrote of how those who obtained certificates of being de-Nazified – cleared of charges of complicity – could and did go out and secure high positions, even though more than a few had been murderers, torturers or willing accomplices. Jaspers mentioned the wellknown case of Hans Globke, who, although not a party member himself, wrote the legal commentary on the Nuremberg race laws, and yet was a trusted aide of Chancellor Adenauer for a full decade after the war. (Karl Jaspers, Wohin treibt die Bundesrepublik? Munich 1966)

In 1949, forty-three percent of the Bavarian state government and eighty-three percent of its district attorneys consisted of people who had been affiliated with the Nazi party. At that time, forty percent of the German population thought Nazism had been "a good idea carried out badly," and in 1950 thirteen percent of the population said they would still vote for the Nazi party. (Frank Stern, The Whitewashing of the Yellow Badge: Anti-Semitism and Philo-Semitism in Postwar Germany, Oxford 1992)

The decade following the war saw Germany cut in two. The German Democratic Republic had little trouble facing a past it claimed not to have. In the west, people threw themselves into rebuilding their cities, their lives and the economy. Reflecting, discussing or imparting knowledge to children about past deeds was simply avoided.

Yiddish singing group Michaele Schoen and Group at Berlin's Hackesche Höfe.
March 1995.

This is not to minimize the moral leadership of the first generation of the Federal Repulic's politicians. At a time when Germans knew they had become the pariah of the western world, when their entire belief system lay in ruins, a few courageous souls set about giving a shattered society something it had entirely lost: a sense of ethics. According to Jeffrey Herf, who has written much and well on the Federal Republic's history, "Theodor Heuss [first president of the Federal Republic], Kurt Schumacher [the SPD party leader imprisoned for a decade by the Nazis] and a host of lesser known figures began the *Vergangenheitsbewältigung* [coming to terms with the past] and were not afraid to draw lessons." Herf added, "These were the people who set a moral tone for the country at a time it was desperately needed, and Adenauer, to a lesser extent, also has to be included." Chancellor Adenauer's wife Gussie died in 1948 as a result of being imprisoned by the Gestapo.

Aside from the politicians themselves, there was also a determined core of West German judges who worked, often against the tide, to bring Nazi criminals to justice. Those in the Justice Department in Ludwigsburg, who processed hundred of cases, worked to abolish the twenty year statute of limitations on presecuting Nazi criminals. (Jeffrey Herf, The Nazi Past and the Two Germanys. Harvard 1996)

During the years of the *Wirtschaftswunder* (the economic miracle), millions of Germans became readers of the right-of-center *Bild Zeitung* and other publications owned by Axel Springer. For many years, these papers played down politics and featured short, perky stories about poor old ladies and cuddly animals, but among the fluff Springer papers paradoxically served-up staunchly *pro*-Israel politics, so much so its journalists had to sign a pledge stating they would not write articles against the Jewish state and his papers remained so after his death in the late 1980s.

Extreme right-wing political parties such as the Nationale Volkspartei rose and fell over the ensuing decades, capturing a foothold in regional parliaments here and there, but they lost them soon after. None could build a national consensus.

Jewish cemeteries and old age homes were defaced on occasion, but by and large, it seemed clear throughout the 1960s that the Federal Republic was turning into a stable democracy, and its industrial-based, export-driven economy was keeping its workers employed, well-fed and content with democracy – a first in Germany's history. But as for relations toward Jews, the Holocaust, and facing the past, these topics remained sealed.

In 1967, Alexander and Margarethe Mitscherlich published *The Inability to Mourn*, (*Die Unfähigkeit zu Trauern*), a ground-breaking study that assessed the national psyche. "The refusal to mourn is most frequent when the losses in question are irretrievable and are the source of excruciating pain on the one hand and shame and anxiety on the other," Margarethe Mitscherlich summarized later in an article. "We fend off the memory of the inhuman sufferings undergone by the millions of victims because to this day Nazi Germany's mass extermination drive fills us not only with shame but also – if we allow these feelings to assert themselves – with immeasurable horror; and it represents a massive assault on our self-respect as Germans."

By the time the Mitscherlichs published their book, however, the seal was beginning to crack. Student protests shook US and European college campuses in 1968, but in Germany, the generation of 1968 also started asking other questions: the questions their parents and grandparents had hoped never to hear or answer: "And what, Dad, did you do during the war? And for whom, grandmother, did you vote?"

"When I asked my grandparents about the war," Thomas Pelzer, a Cologne actor said, "they said I didn't love them and how could I ask such questions. No one – at least many people – wants to hear that from their own family, and so the questions stopped."

But the reaction to the silence did not stop. And if there was still an inability to mourn, there was no longer an inability to criticize and question. For the first time, the rigidity of the German classroom began to be questioned. The all-intimidating power of *der Professor* was no longer so absolute. The Do Not Walk or Sit on the Grass signs in the parks were confronted and in effect, thrown out. Authority – in and of itself – was no longer sacrosanct and German society was changing, some said for the first time since the Bismarck years. A few joked that it was the Americanization of German society that was doing this, that the *Amis*, as they were called, had taught the Germans how to uncross their legs.

Some young Germans went much farther than uncrossing their legs. They chucked bombs and shot people. The activities of the far left Red Army Faction, which wanted to bring down the German government altogether, resorted to bomb attacks, kidnapping and murder, and the government reacted by putting tanks on street corners and police checks and road-blocks throughout the land. A larger percentage of the left, reacting to their parents' closet anti-Semitism and *Bild*-induced pro-Israelism, threw themselves into Middle East politics by wholeheartedly supporting the Palestinian cause. Their anti-Israel rhetoric rang remarkably similar to the Third Reich's own anti-Semitic tirades. Henryk Broder, a Jewish journalist, pointed out how a left-wing travel guide to Israel describes Jews almost identically to Josef Goebbels' propaganda. Others were more sensitive. In 1970, West Germany's first Social Democratic Party chancellor, Willy Brandt, made an official visit to Poland. Standing before the monument to the Jewish ghetto resistance fighters, who took on the wartime German Army even though they were doomed, moved Brandt suddenly to drop to his knees. This was a stunning act of contrition. This was the photo seen round the world. At home, it hit young people especially hard.

Students listening to a lecture at the Patterns of Jewish Life exhibition. January 1992.

Brass band in traditional Bavarian costume about to play at a commemoration service at the Dachau concentration camp. May 1993.

Federal Republic could reach back to earlier imperial times in an unbroken continuum. This, he said, did not, and could not, work. Soon a vigorous debate, which raged heatedly for two years, filled books, magazines and conferences. In the end, Nolte found it difficult to find respectable publishing houses to print his historical theories which became more and more bizarre.

During the weeks prior to and after the fiftieth anniversary of *Kristallnacht* in 1988, articles about Jews, Germans and the Holocaust flooded the newspapers to a degree never before seen. Books were released, television documentaries ran on all channels, and there were major exhibitions in several cities as well as the opening of several Jewish museums and Nazi period study centers throughout the country. It seemed that the entire society was super-sensitve to things Jewish. When the president of the *Bundestag*, Philip Jenninger, delivered a bumbling speech about German guilt that was deemed as inappropiate, he was forced to resign.

Exactly one year later, on the fifty-first anniversary of *Kristallnacht*, the Berlin Wall was toppled, changing the face of Germany – and the history of Europe. But even the euphoria of German unification failed to stop the country's obsession with its recent past. Exhibitions on Jewish life, public podium discussions and magazine articles would only grow in number during the years after reunification, despite yet more dire predictions that a big Germany would be a forgetful Germany.

More Klezmer musicians were now playing in Germany than in the US. There was even a Klezmer workshop, put on by a band called Harry's Freilach for those who wanted to better learn the flavor, whatever that meant. In Berlin in 1992, when the blockbuster exhibition, "Patterns of Jewish Life" (*Jüdische Lebenswelten*) in the Martin-Gropius-Bau attracted 350,000 visitors in four months. In a city that then had less than 10,000 Jews, one could hardly say it was geared solely toward them.

By 1995, the fact that people had danced on the Wall six years earlier got not more than a big 'So What' of a shrug. German unification was celebrated on October third, and with it came a bank holiday. November ninth remained as the day Germans commemorated *Kristallnacht*, not the fall of communism. Another memorial day was added to the calendar: January twenty-seventh, the day the Soviet Army liberated Auschwitz.

By 1996, according to Monika Richarz, former head of the Leo Baeck Institute in New York and now director of the Institute for the History of German Jews in Hamburg, more than one thousand books on Jewish history and culture were being published each year, in German. "We have seen Jewish museums literally sprouting up all over this country," she said. "Ten years ago, I welcomed invitations to conferences in Germany on Jewish history and went to every one. Now I turn down far more offers than I receive. There are just too many." Shuffling through the papers on her desk, she pulled out a brochure on a soon to open Jewish museum going up in Halberstadt, then another paper on a Jewish studies department at the university of Braunschweig. Other brochures peeked out of the pile. Rendsburg was rebuilding a synagogue. Giessen had literally moved a synagogue from a village nearby. She handed me a brochure from the Central Archive on Jewish history in Germany, which was now operating in Heidelberg.

In her own institute, founded in 1966 to create a study center for pre-war Hamburg Jewry, more than one hundred students from the university attend classes and lectures annually. In Berlin, there is a Department of Jewish Studies at the Free University as well as an Institute for Anti-Semitic Studies at the Technical University. Together, they have seen nearly one thousand students. More recently, Julius Schoeps left his post in Duisburg to open the Moses Mendelssohn Center in Potsdam, thirty kilometers south of town. There are also Jewish studies programs in Cologne and Frankfurt.

"This is not to say there is not a strain of anti-Semitism in Germany today," Richarz cautioned. "There is, absolutely. Look at the neo-Nazi violence of the past few years. And yes, you can make the point that Germans are interested in the past, or as some have put it indelicately, dead Jews. But they are studying, they are learning. And I figure: why fight the interest?"

In the Sachsenhausen concentration camp museum, visitors ponder an exhibition on the history of Anti-Semitism. September 1995.

How deep this interest goes in German society is difficult to measure. More than seventy sister city relationships operate between the Israel and Germany. Choirs, symphonies and sports clubs are shunted back and forth. Neither the Israeli Embassy in Bonn nor the German Embassy in Tel Aviv could provide me with the number of German-Israeli friendship societies (well over a hundred, they both estimated). Yet many of these organizations are run by people in their sixties or older and they claim that few younger Germans are joining these days.

The three major German political parties all maintain offices in Israel and they support programs in various universities plus Arab-Israeli dialogue groups. They also ship scholars, students and technicians to Germany to study there. All will admit, however, that many scholarships for German studies go begging, unfulfilled.

A vigorous exchange program continually sends German and Israel politicians to each others countries and not just on a parliamentary level. The *Zentralwohlfahrtsstelle der Juden in Deutschland* (Central Welfare Council of Jews in Germany) arranges tours of Israeli schools for teachers from the former East Germany as well as social workers. Bennie Bloch, director of *ZWST*, said, "We figure that since Israel has so much experience in dealing with new immigrants, we may as well share the knowledge since Jews from the former Soviet Union are now coming to Germany."

A variety of organizations such as the Atlantic Brücke and the Bertelsmann Foundation hold conferences on Israeli-German relations, while Israeli embassy workers in Bonn and their colleagues in Berlin travel the length and breadth of the Federal Republic giving lectures, opening exhibitions and meeting with university students. It is not uncommon, for instance, for Jaakov Seefer-Vismunski, Israel's Berlin consul, to give ten speeches in four cities in a week.

Zvi Liran, director of the Israel Government Tourist Office, said over a quarter million Germans visited Israel in 1995. For a country with 80 million people, this is enormous compared to 500,000 visitors from Canada and the United States combined. Most did little more than get sunburned in Eilat and had their pictures taken bobbing in the Dead Sea, but a great many visited Jewish sites, including Yad Vashem, Israel's Holocaust museum. This is where I ran into Erich Spier, a protestant pastor from Berlin, who tries to bring as many former East Germans to Israel as possible. "They know so little," he said as he watched a group of teachers from Potsdam walk through Yad Vashem. "For many of them, this is their first brush with the truth."

American Jewish groups are also favored by the German political establishment. The American Jewish Committee, B'nai B'rith and Hillel work in conjunction with the political foundations, the Federal Press and Information Agency and the quasi-governmental *Inter Nationes*. Members of these organizations are invited to Germany as guests to meet politicians, school groups and sociologists. They also tour concentration camps. In recent years I have run into German-sponsored tours for Jewish museum directors, the Chicago board of Rabbis, the Presidents of American Jewish Organizations and editors of Jewish newspapers. Obviously these tours are, to be diplomatic, meant to sow seeds of understanding and provide outsiders with a broader view of Germany, although Gerhard Wahlers, who handled American Jewish visits for the Konrad Adenauer Foundation before moving on to their Israel office, said, "Well, let's be honest. Every party has its own interests."

Surveys of attitudes toward Israel and Jews are constantly taken in Germany. According to an American Jewish Committee/Emnid Poll released in April 1994, twenty-two percent of Germans wouldn't want a Jew for a neighbor. But even more didn't want Africans, Poles, Turks, Vietnamese, Arabs or Gypsies next door. Eleven percent of West Germans didn't even want an East German neighbor. Twenty percent said Jews have too much influence on society and over half agreed with the statement that "we should not talk so much about the Holocaust." Yet twenty-six percent feel that anti-Semitism is a very serious problem in Germany and forty-six percent feared it would increase.

Helmut Kohl, too, learned from the stumbles made earlier in his chancellorship. Ever the master-politician, he saw little need in addressing issues about the past to large audiences of German voters. Yet it was a beaming Helmut Kohl who looked on in Jerusalem in Juni 1995, as Hebrew University students and teachers dedicated a European study center in his name. Six month later, at a B'nai B'rith dinner in Munich in January 1996, Kohl seemed to speak from the heart, of how the synagogue in his home town was burned when he was a boy, and of how some Jews were brave enough to rebuild Jewish life in Germany after the war – and continued to do so now.

Monuments and memorials commemorating the war and the Holocaust have been built, and continue to be built, throughout the country. Some are controversial in their design, a few have the power to emotionally move visitors; others do not. More to the point, one would accuse the Germans of ignoring the past altogether if they were not there at all.

Some monuments blur the lines of guilt and responsibility uncomfortably. In Berlin, in the newly reconstructed *Neue Wache* war memorial, there the words are written on its walls: "To the victims of fascist and terrorist regimes." Yet almost across the street, on the site where Josef Goebbels saw books written by Jews burn in a bonfire in 1933, there is a chilling monument – one looks down through a glass manhole to see an underground room of white, empty bookshelves.

Few monuments have the emotional power of the simple signs that were placed around Berlin's *Bayerisches Viertel*, where middle class Jews once lived. Here, on a sign hanging from a lamp post just in front of a park bench, is a painting of a bench, on the other side is written the date when Jews could no longer sit on them. A few meters away, just before a bank entrance, a sign informs passersby when Jews were forbidden to enter. Such signs, scores of them, lace the entire area – with reminders before bakeries, grocery stores, hospitals. Residents shop, children play, clerks open and close their stores, just as their Jewish neighbors had done alongside them, before their rights, then their lives, were taken away.

Teachers from Potsdam in Yad Vashem in Jerusalem. January 1995.

Kristallnacht commemoration in the People's Chamber, the East German Parliament. November 1988.

German tourists at the Holocaust Museum Yad Vashem in Israel.
October 1993.

Ignatz Bubis, chairman of the Central Council of Jews in Germany, with Chancellor Helmut Kohl, at the dedication ceremony of the Centrum Judaicum, Berlin.
May 1995.

Page 66/67
In the US Holocaust Memorial Museum. March 1995.

From Object to Subject

The Germans had come to Poland to care for dead Jews. The Polish Jews had come to see how the Germans were doing it. And Marc Fisher of the Washington Post and I had come along to see how the two groups interacted.

In June 1993, twenty-eight volunteers from the Action Reconciliation bureau in Berlin took it upon themselves in June 1993 to repair the forlorn and neglected Jewish cemetery of Szprotawa, a non-descript town in forlorn and neglected north-western Silesia, now in Poland. This is a region that had been part of Germany since the Prussians swiped it from the Poles in the 1700s. Ethnically mixed over the centuries among Germans, Poles and Jews, the Germans chased out or murdered the Jews and Poles during the Third Reich. When Stalin moved Poland's borders westward in 1945, the Poles chased the Germans out. To resettle this de-populated land, Poles from eastern Poland,

Nadja März, a volunteer with Action Reconciliation, helping clean up the Jewish cemetery in Szprotawa, Poland.

A German volunteer with Action Reconciliation listening to Moses Grin.

which had been doubly ethnically cleansed when it was swallowed by the Soviet Union, (now Ukraine and Belorussia) were offered homes in Silesia and Pommerania.

Among those who came were Mauricy Kailer and his wife, and Moses Grin, three Jews who escaped the fate of their families by fleeing eastward toward Siberia during the War. They, like some 10,000 other Jews, remained in Poland throughout the postwar period, despite the country's occasional outbursts of anti-Semitism. Along with a hundred or so other elderly Jews, they lived in nearby Zary. Every one of them was a transplant from Galicia, to the east.

Mauricy Kailer was an imposing man. Dressed in a three piece suit, a fedora and a trench coat draped around his shoulders, even at eighty-four-years old he stood tall, though he propelled himself along with the aid of a rough-hewn wooden cane. He and his wife and Grin, leaders of the Zary community, had come to inspect the work of Action Reconciliation. The elderly Jews looked over the efforts the Germans were making at the Szprotawa cemetery, cutting trees, mowing grass, repairing fences, and resurrecting fallen Jewish gravestones. They commended the work, and agreed to chat with the Germans at the guest house where they were staying.

While a vegetarian dinner was being prepared in the downstairs kitchen, Torsten Schramm, leader of the Action Reconciliation Group, arranged chairs in a circle. Torsten began by saying that it was important for the Jews of Zary to understand why Action Reconciliation had come, and what they hoped to achieve. Kailer and Grin shrugged and smiled.

"My father was in the SS," Torsten told the three Jews whose family had been murdered by the Nazis. "I wrote a book about our relationship and I have been working very intensively on the German past." He went on to talk about those things the German left held dear: the peace movement and the need for Germans to face their past by actually working to atone for the sins of their fathers. Action Reconciliation operated in every country that had been a victim of the Third Reich, and they had also worked alongside Cesar Chavez and the United Farm Workers in California. He waited for Kailer to respond. The old man just kept smiling.

Barbara Schultze's parents had also been Nazis. Reluctant to speak but anxious to say something, she asked Kailer if there was anything she and her friends could do for them.

The old Jew said no and patted her hand. Then there was silence. So Torsten began again and told the visitors about other programs of Action Reconciliation, of their work in Holocaust museums in the United States and of their projects in Israel. Then again, silence.

Kailer, leathery hands wrapped around his cane before him, cleared his throat. Forming the words slowly, he said in a deep and gravely voice, *"Ich bin in Österreich geboren,"* (I was born in Austria). There came a pause and a wry smile, then *"in einer Kaiserlich und Königlichen Stadt namens Lemberg"* (in the royal and imperial city Lemberg – now Lviv in Ukraine). With these few words, the eighty-four-year-old man, who had been writing for the last remaining Yiddish newspaper in Poland for half a century – sometimes fiction, other times news – transported himself back to the time when Emperor Franz Josef I ruled the Austro-Hungarian Empire, which stretched from the shores of the Adriatic to Polish Galicia. He talked of a time when millions of Jews kept the Emperor's portrait in their homes, of the vitality of Jewish life, literature and culture throughout the empire, how Jews were not only living in impoverished shtetls, but going off to universities in Prague and Vienna to learn, create, write, build. How he and his friends argued politics and took sides, became socialists, communists, Zionists, capitalists. Kailer paused for a moment, and then added that when this century was born, the Jews of the Empire looked forward to a future that would be as bright and promising as the previous fifty years had been.

It was not to be. The elderly emperor died during the First World War, his empire was carved up by successor states that turned into enemies, chaos prevailed, and then came Hitler. Mauricy Kailer, sitting in a room full of well-meaning young German leftists, spoke of lost hopes, destroyed worlds and extinguished lives of the Jews of Central Europe, *Mitteleuropa.* His friends were murdered, their homes destroyed, even the traces of their lives were now gone. He spoke softly, his eyes looking back at the world that he could obviously still feel. "You see," he said as he scanned the room, "we really are the last of the Mohicans." He patted his wife's hand. Moses Grin smiled slightly and looked down at the floor. I thought, everyone must have been as spellbound as I was.

A hand shot up, and in a cheerful voice, a perky blonde German woman said, "I would like to tell you about our march against the Pershing missiles in Bonn back in 1983. It's where most of us in this room first met."

Kailer smiled indulgently. Neither the Jews, who survived the destruction of their world, nor the young Germans, offspring of those who destroyed it, were talking to each other. Before the old Jews drove home across the meadows and the abandoned German farms of northwestern Silesia, Torsten and his friends sang Shalom Aleichem and thanked them for coming.

Beatrix Kirchhofer, who studied nursing in her home town Freiburg, had never considered joining a group like Action Reconciliation. She had been on holiday in Israel in 1994, back-packing here and there, and exploring the country by bus. She became intrigued enough with the Jewish state, and with her own feelings as a German toward the past, to want to do something – not through a church or a peace group, but directly. She talked it over with her parents. "Do it," her mother told her. "And try to give the impression there are some good Germans out there."

Beatrix, twenty-eight years old, set about writing letters to old age homes throughout Israel, seeking to work there as a volunteer. Most did not respond, or they wrote back to say they had no need for volunteers. But Miriam Shetreet, a social worker at the predominantly German-Jewish Siegfried Moses Home in Jerusalem, responded immediately. Many of the residents in the home suffered strokes and dementia, their Hebrew dropped off and they retreated into their mother tongue. It used to be easier to find an offspring of a German Jew, like Miriam herself. But now it was next to impossible to find Israeli nurses who spoke German, and Miriam Shetreet kept an eye out for letters such as the one that landed on her desk from Freiburg. In the winter of 1995, as snow caked the mountains surrounding her hometown, Beatrix flew to Israel, threw herself into learning Hebrew, and went to work at the Siegfried Moses Old Age Home for the next eight months.

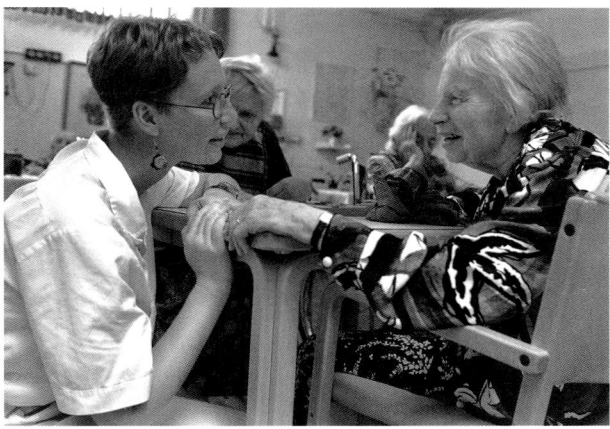

Beatrix Kirchhofer, from Freiburg, working as a volunteer in the Siegfried Moses Old Age Home in Jerusalem. May 1995.

"I suppose I had built up some defenses, because I did not expect that when I, a German nurse, walked into this home, that I would be very warmly welcomed," she told me as she readied her nurses station one morning. "I mean, I came because I wanted to come and I guess I focused on the fact this was necessary. I simply forgot – no, I didn't know – how nice everyone would be. I know it's probably a cliché, but Jewish people are so warm and friendly." She blushed a little. "Not exactly as we are at home." She suppressed a giggle, then hurried after one of her charges, Frau Sonnenblum from Graz, who had a tendency to wander off and get lost and upset.

The following morning I accompanied Beatrix on her rounds. She began downstairs, where those in need of constant care lay in their beds or sat in the armchairs next to them. There were pills to administer, eyes and noses to clean, drops and injections to give and salves to rub. Upstairs, Beatrix wheeled around her medicine cart. When she entered a room, a smile flashed, hands rubbed together in happiness. "You look so lovely," she told one patient. "You're certainly getting better," she said to another. There were conversations here and there, and a few old ones wrapped their liver-spotted hands around hers.

It was intense work, and it went on from 7:00 AM until lunch time. "I don't feel guilty for the past, but I'm here because I feel responsible," Beatric Kirchhofer said, "I mean, it happened in Germany and I'm a German. That's a simple equation. I'm not proud to be a German, and in any case, I didn't build a country from the ground up. But the people here, the ones who were chased out of Germany, they did come here, they did work, and I know it's kitsch to say, but they made the desert bloom. Well they did! Now that's something you can be proud of." She peered outside. A foursome was just preparing to play a game of bridge. "But when they speak of the past, especially the ones who were in the camps, I can hardly bear it. Some want to talk about it. Some have to talk about it. And there are times when I feel so awful that after I leave them, I go down in the nurse's station and I just sob and cry and I swear I can't go on and I wonder, what have I gotten myself into here? She stopped and listened, then looked outside. "It's Mrs. Sonnenblum again," she sighed. "I think I'd better go and chat with her a while."

Schmetterling
aller Wesen gute Nacht
Die Gewichte von Leben und Tod
senken sich mit deinen Flügeln
auf die Rose nieder
die mit heimwärts reifendem Licht welk.

Nelly Sachs

Back to school

It was the kind of request I immediately turn down. The city theater of Schwerin, a former East German town north of Berlin in Mecklenburg-Vorpommern, wanted to hang prints from my first photographic study of Jews in East Central Europe during their presentation of Fiddler on the Roof. The request had come to me through the American consulate in Berlin and I responded with a gut level "No."

But a few nights later, Nicu Merc, a west Berlin dramatist working in the Schwerin Theater, came and told me why he wanted my work, "Because they simply don't know anything about Jews there, and your exhibition, of children and parents and real life – today – helps break the Fiddler on the Roof stereotype. If we can bring school children through to see the pictures – and hopefully meet you so you can talk to them about it, then we will have accomplished something."

I changed my mind on the spot. After all, I was curious to know what German school children were learning about the past, the Holocaust, and Jews. I was being offered a chance to learn, so I grabbed it, and a few weeks later, stepped off the train on a drizzly winter morning.

Schwerin had not been badly bombed during the Second World War, nor did the GDR lavish much Stalinist-era heavy industry on it. That left it almost perfectly intact, and after 1989, the town threw itself into a renovation program that, as the scaffolding came down and the paint brushes were put away, exposed as charming and elegant a town

Poem by the Jewish poet Nelly Sachs given out during Name Day at the school now bearing her name in Köpenick.

center as any as I had seen in Central Europe. As Merc promised, my photographs had been hung throughout the Schwerin Theater and several schools sent classes by. I spent the better part of a day there, and each group was unfailingly courteous, each presented me with a small bouquet of flowers. I gave the same talk I usually do: that Jewish life exists in all East Central Europe, despite the best efforts of Germany to wipe it out during the War. That the traditional, old-fashioned, orthodox world of the Eastern European Jew exists no more, except in pockets in Antwerp, New York, Jerusalem and a few other places. But there are still Jews in Hungary, Bulgaria and the Czech and Slovak Republics who are proud of their roots and religion and proud to be Hungarians, Bulgarians, Czechs and Slovaks as well.

Questions came as they would from teenagers. Boys asked about my cameras and was it true that in Israel, everyone had a gun; the girls asked about intermarriage and what the word kosher meant. I was, after all, the first living Jew these kids had ever seen.

A few weeks later I was invited back to speak at the local high school. I was so enthusiastic that I phoned a reporter friend, Ute Frings, who writes for one of Germany's national left-of-center daily newspapers, the *Frankfurter Rundschau*. Together we left Berlin by train on another grey and drizzly morning and were met by the theater's public relations officer, Petra Haacke. She greeted us cheerfully but would end up rueing this day.

At the school, I first met with a group of twelve year olds. I showed slides, I told stories, I spoke of Jewish customs and traditions. As only the young can do (when they wish to) they listened spellbound. As soon as they could, they practically wiggled out of their chairs, eager to ask those remarkable questions that make you fall in love with their innocence.

"Well, I mean, like, just how do I tell a Jew on the street?" asked one lovely blonde girl.

"And Jews don't believe in Jesus – at all?" asked another boy. He asked standing up. When I said Jews thought of him as a great teacher, but not The Savior, he sat down with a plop.

"Why do most of the Jews have beards in Fiddler on the Roof?"

"Is that why you have a beard?"

"Do you have to have one?"

"What happens if you don't eat kosher?" one asked after I explained what that was. "Do you get in really big trouble?"

I would have been glad to have spent the entire day with them, but all too soon, the bell rang. One boy, who had been listening with utmost seriousness and had written down copious notes, ended the session. "Okay, I've heard everything. So tell me, how do I become a Jew?"

After lunch, Ute and I stepped into a classroom of seventeen year olds. I began by posing the same question to them that I had done in other high schools in western Germany, and it had always proven to be an effective conversation starter. Until today.

"Let's begin by talking about a basic difference about how Jews and Germans see the same issue. The year is 1940 and my question to you is, what would you do – for instance, do you think you would hide or turn in a Jew?"

Silence, but not just ordinary silence. This was sullen, angry teenage silence. I pointed to one youngster. "Dunno," he mumbled and glared down at the floor. I encouraged a young girl who was just combing her hair to answer. "No, I doubt it," she said with hostility in her voice, not responding either way.

"Well, would you say that I am asking you an ethical question? A question about morals?"

I saw one nod.

"Then please, now you ask me. What would you be doing in the war?" Silence.

I sighed. "Well it's an easy question to answer –

I'd be dead. Or if not dead, running from you. You see, this is the major difference – you, as Germans, can look on the Holocaust period and think of it as a horrible crime, and you would wonder of the ethics and morals involved, and how they relate to you today. But no Jew looks at the Holocaust as an ethical issue. It is a matter of survival. It is the ultimate nightmare.

Absolutely no sign of intelligent life. I soldiered on.

As I spoke and showed slides, girls combed their hair, boys slept, others did homework or passed pieces of paper back and forth. All the while, Ute Frings scribbled away. When I posed questions to them, there were mumbled, inaudible replies. Have you ever met a Jew? Silence. Seen a Jew? Silence. On television? Silence. So I'm your first victim? Blank stares.

Anyone know what a synagogue is? Silence. A rabbi? Silence. As I clicked through the slides, I stopped at one: "Here's a picture called 'Dresden synagogue with Trabant,' (the tiny, plastic car East Germans drove). There were no smiles or laughs. Instead, eyes rolled and heads shook. Finally the bell rang. One girl audibly said, "Thank God," gathered her books and shuffled out of the room with her friends. Only then did one student come up and ask me why I thought the Germans had killed so many Jews. Anyone who poses a question in such a way already has the answer. "Why don't you tell me," I said. And he did. "Because the Jews were smarter and better at business and the Germans felt they just had to get rid of them.

"But mass murder?"

"Sure," he shrugged. "I mean, I guess they felt they had to. Or...oh, I don't know." Then he shuffled off.

The teacher apologized. "I'm sorry they didn't pay better attention." I replied that I speak to scores of groups every year and that some are interested, some are not.

We took the train home to Berlin and Ute wrote up her story and recorded exactly what she saw (the dialogue above was pulled from her article). Two days later, on the twenty-first of January 1993, nearly a quarter million Germans opened their paper to read of how fresh and frisky the younger students were, and how the older class responded.

And a cry went up in Schwerin. The school director nearly exploded. He demanded that Ute Frings return to Schwerin to face the class and its teacher to explain herself. And while her fist reaction was to laugh it off, she was too intrigued to say no. I went along.

We were given a place along a long conference table in a closed room. Across from us sat the teacher, the school director and students. Every student brought along a photo-copy of Ute's article, covered with highlighter marks, red pen underlinings and pages upon pages of notes and comments.

The school director told us how deeply shocked he was, and how awful and untruthful the article was. Worse, he said, the school would now refuse all contacts with journalists in the future. Even though a major television network had asked to come to their school, the answer, for them and from now on, was No! He turned his head to the side and sniffed the air. He was finished with the likes of us.

Class of twelve year olds in the former East German city of Schwerin. January 1993.

The teacher then spoke. With a trembling voice, she said she felt Ute Frings had betrayed them. Until that article appeared, she had been thinking of creating a trip to Israel for the kids, but now... now... and she exploded into tears. Students fluttered around her and stared daggers at Ute.

Then they lashed out. "Why did you write that there is rust on the side of the school?"

"Because it's there?" replied Ute

"And why did you write there is swastika in the town?"

"Because it's also there." Acutally, she wrote that "there was a dialogue in graffiti, with Nazis Out! on one side of the street and the Swastika across from it."

Then turning to me, one student attacked, her mouth twisting with derision as she spoke, "Well Mr. Serotta, we were completely bored during your talk and for a very good reason. You are boring, your talk was boring, and we in the former GDR know everthing about Jews. After all, we've been to Buchenwald!"

At this I could have, and perhaps should have, laughed. Or I simply could have replied that what they learned about history in general and the Holocaust specifically was, at best, inadequate and at worst, dangerously off the mark. But I held my tongue.

"That's right," chimed in another, finding it safer now that someone else had attacked first. "You are really boring to us. Boring! Ha!"

What they were railing against was nothing specifically Jewish, anti-Jewish or anything of the sort. What enraged the students and teachers was that a national newspaper ran a story that showed they had acted like a bunch of bored and none-too-inquisitive teenagers. That is one thing. Filled with that pervasive inferiority complex and rage East Germans have against the arrogant West Germans, they simply exploded.

It was ugly and it was impotent, because for them, the damage was done. See how the west looks at us was all they could conjure. Not untypically, they refused to see any fault in themselves whatsoever. I was boring, Ute was evil and they were wronged.

As the two of us sat facing each other in the train heading back to Berlin, we tried to laugh it off, but we were really just licking our wounds. I vowed that I would never, ever, speak to a school class in Germany again.

The next day the phone rang. "My name is Budemeier, I'm calling from the Waldorfschule in Bremen and I want to talk to Mr. Serotta." My first reaction: play the Chinese houseboy and say he's gone 'til next year. But I said it was me. This Mr. Budemeier said he read with "great interest" the story of my Schwerin fiasco, that the students in their school were just then learning about Jewish history and they'd like me to come speak to them. I said I would really have to think about it but I'd probably say no.

He said he really hoped I would say yes. After all, they had asked the Bremen Jewish community to come and speak but there had been no interest. Anyway, they were studying Jews in Eastern Europe and a slide talk by me would really be perfect.

Hoping to discourage him, for the very first time, I told a school that I would have to charge a fee. Okay, he said, if I wanted DM 500 they would pay it, plus my travel expenses.

"All right already", I said, "I'll do it". I agreed to meet this Mr. Budemeier on the front steps of the school in a few weeks at 11:00 AM. (One thing for sure: I wasn't telling that damned Ute Frings.)

I stepped out of the taxi in front of the school just at the appointed hour, but the only souls gathered on the steps were an outcrop of gangly teenagers standing around doing nothing. The tallest and gangliest among them looked over to me. "Can I help you?"

"No thanks, I'm waiting for Mr. Budemeier."

"I'm Mr. Budemeier."

I stopped dead. Oh please no, I thought.

"You? You're Mr. Budemeier?"

He smiled. "Sure. You can call me Phillip."

I can call you worse than that, I thought to myself as he led me into the school. I could picture it now: some kid has asked me to speak, the teachers won't know a damn thing about it, and I'm going to either get laughed out or thrown out of the school and probably both.

"Let me have your slides," he said and gave it to a pony tailed, ear-ringed youth who trotted ahead. Scores of kids were heading toward the auditorium. Inside I stopped short. Before me were two hundred-fifty to three hundred chairs – all filled, a slide screen and projector already set up. The teachers standing against the far wall.

One teacher explained everthing to me. This was a school for advanced students and in Waldorf schools, the children create and carry out their own programs. This whole event was Phillip's idea. I would have heard more, but Phillip came over and told me that first there would be a short speech

about Jews in Eastern Europe and the Holocaust. Then there would be a choral reading by a group of the oldest boys. Then I would be on. He dashed off.

A girl read from a prepared paper. She spoke for some ten minutes, covered most of the right historical bases and ended by saying that the Jewish life that existed pre-war was no more. And that was due to Germany, she said.

Then the boys shuffled into place. One stepped out and stood before them, and raising his hand,

Student performers on Name Day at the Nelly Sachs School in Köpenick, Berlin. December 1993.

they began. In almost a shout, but in perfet unison, they recited Paul Celan's 'Todesfuge' (Death Fugue) – four years after I had heard it for the first time on the German press bus in Poland.

This I was not prepared for, nor had I ever heard these powerful words declaimed in such fashion. The boys' loud, clipped, clear voices – nearly shouting – were devastatingly effective. I knew then, and said it to myself, that if I live a long long time, I would always remember this moment.

Taking a half minute to collect myself, I stood before the students. I took a deep breath and began. "Okay, so the year is 1940, and... "

When I started with the slides, someone yelled, "Try English. We all speak it!" Happily, I complied and I went through my talk on Romania, Bulgaria and elsewhere, and spoke of Jews, Nazism, Communism. I could feel the interest this time was real and as I went along, I dropped the occasional joke. And miracle of miracles, they got it. They laughed.

In Germany! I went on, joked a bit more when it was appropriate, and finished up nearly an hour later. With the house lights up, as the flood of questions came, I looked to see that my speakers fee was being collected by the students from the students. And I finished by telling them that this had been the most riveting morning I had spent in Germany, and that in appreciation, I would accept my fee, but it would go directly to the Sarajevo Jewish community, which was then helping its Christian and Muslim neighbors. The applause came loud and long, and I think if they had offered me a teaching position then, I would have stayed.

As I sat in the warmth of the restaurant car on the Berlin bound train that afternoon and swirled a spoon around in my soup, I thought: German schools, back to back. One east, the other west. One was a quite normal high school, suffering unter the burden of parents without jobs, a radical rewrite of its curricula and the other school rich, its students the cream of the crop. Of course there could be no comparison, nor should there be. And if I had discovered anything about what Germans were learning about the past, I knew I would have to stop lumping them together. And as for what East German students were learning, not all have proved to be as hostile as those in Schwerin.

Köpenick is a pleasant red-brick factory town sandwiched between the Dahme river and the Müggelsee on the southern tip of eastern Berlin. Submerged behind the Wall during the communist decades, Köpenick began scrubbing itself clean after 1989. During the changeover, one of the technical schools became a high school. Six hundred students attended class there, and one of the first projects to practice their newly-received democracy was to find a proper name for the school. Students were told that they would have to decide, and they were told to choose a name carefully because it would be a lasting one. Some said that with the scores of high schools in Berlin, all the good ones had already been taken. And what the world did not need was another Goethe, Schiller or Lessing school.

At the end of a week, at a gathering of several classes, the name of Gustave Harz, a Nobel Prize winning physicist was floated by one student. A few nods of approval. Herlaine Stocke, a writer, was suggested by someone else. A couple more nods. What about John Lennon, someone else said. There were some giggles, but then, why not? Friederike Jennrich, fourteen years old, raised her hand. She had a suggestion – Nelly Sachs. Who? Someone asked.

"Nelly Sachs", Friederike repeated.

"I looked her up," Friederike told them. "She was Jewish, she was German, she was born here in Berlin, and she won the Nobel Prize for literature in 1966. And there isn't a single school named for her."

"What you must understand," the perky teenager told me later as she leaned over her Snoopy-decorated notebook, "that was back in 1992 and 1993. These were the worst times of the neo-Nazi violence. And a lot of it was right here in the former GDR – Rostock, Hoyerswerda, the murder of a black man on a train. I just felt that naming the school for Nelly Sachs was the right thing to do. Especially then." When Friederike suggested Nelly Sachs that day in class, several students replied, "Stimmt!" (Absolutely!).

Names were formally submitted and a vote came to narrow the field. Sachs would face off Stocke and Harz. Fact sheets were needed for each name, and Friederike volunteered to write the paper on Sachs. She read the biography by Gabriele Fritsch Vivie and wrote the author a letter requesting more information. She saw that Nelly Sachs had been friends with Hans Magnus Enzensberger, so she wrote to Germany's best known living poet as well. Vivie and Enzensberger responded immediately and a few weeks later Friederike presented her report to the school assembly. "I'd like to tell you all about Nelly Sachs," she told the six hundred classmates before her, "and I'd like you to hear this poem."

Butterfly
blessed night of all beings!
The weights of life and death
sink down with your wings
on the rose
which withers with the light ripening
homewards.

(translation: Ruth and Matthew Mead)

In the vote that followed, the students decided by a two-to-one margin that their school would be named for the Berlin Jew, Nelly Sachs. They would send this message to neo-Nazis, and they would commemorate the new name with a special day of programs in honor of Sachs. That day was to be on the thirteenth of December 1993.

To prepare, they studied up on the Holocaust and Jewish history. They invited Berlin Jews who lived through that period to come and address the school, and their invitations were all accepted. They studied Nelly Sachs' work and when Friederike wrote to Enzensberger and asked if he would come to Köpenick to speak of poetry and Sachs, he agreed.

Then Name Day. Norma Drimmer, a vivacious mother of three and member of the Berlin Jewish community's executive board, picked me up early and we drove eastward, past where the wall once stood, past the Soviet Army monument in Treptow, and into Köpenick. Norma, who handled the board's educational programs, had been invited to the school for the event and insisted I come with her. "This is something you might want to see," she told me. "From what I can gather, this is not one of these international high schools, not some school where the famous send their children. This is…" and she searched for the word, "…Köpenick!"

On the day Berlin got its first Nelly Sachs High School, students from that school stood before a crowded auditorium/sports hall and played a Mendelssohn string quartet. Several students stood up and recited the heartfelt, darkly transparent verse of the Jewish woman who escaped her fate, and lived to be torn by guilt ever after.

Students dressed in black shirts and high boots goose-stepped onto the stage, grabbed other students and flung them on the floor and covered them with a large and fluttering plastic sheet – gas. Norma and I looked at each other. And when it was over, she whispered, "I've been to a lot of these things, and to some important and impressive ones, but this one, I'm afraid, got me where it hurts: my heart."

Two years after that Name Day, I sat with Friederike in the school director's office. She was sixteen years old now, with spikey, reddish hair. When I asked her what naming the school for Nelly Sachs had accomplished, she replied, "I know that by naming our school after Nelly Sachs, that her poetry, and the story it tells, will forever be part of our studies here. After my friends and I are not here, new kids will come, and they will start to learn of Nelly Sachs and the Holocaust all over again."

"But what will they learn?" I asked.

She smiled. "Learn – that's a relative word. It means different things to different people – learn what? Well, I hope they learn about the past, about the Holocaust, and that they will be sensitive to it. But not only that. Here in East Germany, we haven't had such a great experience with democracy, and not so much practice. So this is a good place to begin learning about how such a crime as the Holocaust happens, and how that kind of crime can be prevented: by practicing and caring for your democracy. That," she said as she exhaled a deep breath, "is what I hope students will learn."

"Oh yes, and one more thing. Our school class went to Normandy for the fiftieth anniversary of the Allied invasion. Some of the students just didn't care at all, and I felt helpless, because they weren't absorbing the lessons of that place, of that war. But I know this, because I saw it – you can walk across a cemetery, like some kids did at Normandy. But you can't walk across the poems of Nelly Sachs."

Search for Identity

Long before there was a country called Germany, the Jews of Prague, Vienna, Czernowitz, Berlin, Trieste, Zürich, Danzig and Frankfurt wrote, spoke and defined themselves in the German language. They did not move but Europe's borders did. The German states unified under Prussian rule in 1871; Austrian rule collapsed forty-seven years later and a checkerboard of successor states took its place. By the time the map of Central Europe was re-drawn in 1945, few Jews were still alive. What re-mained were the ideas they left behind.

In the half century before their destruction, German-speaking Jews produced a greatness we are still in awe of. Sigmund Freud pioneered the exploration of dreams and the unconscious. One of his patients was Gustav Mahler, who turned angst into symphonies. Franz Kafka's angst-ridden novels presaged Europe's nightmares. And Albert Einstein rewrote modern science. By 1933, thirteen of Germany's thirty-three Nobel prize winners had been of Jewish (or half-Jewish) descent.

In the years prior to and just after the First World War – the Indian summer of German cul-ture, as H. I. Bach calls it – German Jewry also reached its finest hour as it forged a synthesis of modern Judaism. Impassioned Zionists discussed and argued with the great Jewish philosophers of the day. New translations of the Bible and Talmud were published. Lecture halls filled to hear philoso-phers like Franz Rosenzweig, Hermann Cohen and Martin Buber, whose books went into dozens of printings. Berlin's chief rabbi, Leo Baeck, by the very example of being an integrated citizen yet pas-sionately and devoutly Jewish, inspired many of his co-religionists throughout the land. "Through our Jewishness, not away from our Jewishness leads the path to our Humanity," he wrote. But in 1933, with the coming to power of the Nazis, Leo Baeck also wrote that the one thousand year history of German Jewry had come to an end.

German Jewry as it existed then is no more. Leo Baeck was deported from Berlin to Theresien-stadt in 1943. He survived only because there hap-pened to have been another Leo Baeck in the camp and that man was transported to Auschwitz and death. Baeck then settled in London, where he re-mained until his death in 1956. And like Baeck, the great majority of German Jews never returned home.

Between 1945–1948, around a quarter million Jews passed through Germany on their way to other lands. They lived in Displaced Persons camps and ranged from the tens of thousands of Polish Jews fleeing murderous anti-Semitism at home to Romanian, Czech and Hungarian Jews who had survived the concentration camps. Their families had been wiped out and they now had nowhere else to go. Not surprisingly, the leadership of the DP camps wanted to get everyone out of Europe. Zionism was the only answer they could envisage. They called themselves She'erit ha Peletah (the surviving remnant) and agitated constantly for per-mission to enter British-held Palestine. By 1948, with Israel a state, two-thirds headed off to make Zionism a reality while the rest emigrated to Canada, the US and elsewhere. A few, a very few, remained. Leaving the camps, they drifted into rubble-strewn cities to join the tiny number of

Liam's first bar mitzvah lesson with Rabbi Goldberger. May 1996.

German-born Jews who had survived by hiding, or who had returned, claiming they were too old to go anywhere else.

Most Jews told themselves that staying in Germany would not be permanent, only temporary. Until things are better in Israel, they said. Until I'm sure my sister from Poland really died. Until I get my money from the German government. Until I sell my property. Until my sick mother passes away. Until I get that invitation from my brother in Seattle. Until, until... But some did stay. In 1950, some 20,000 Jews were registered in Germany. In 1933 there were more than half a million.

Before the Second World War, Hugo Spiegel had been a cattle dealer in Wahrendorf, a small town in Westphalia. The Spiegel family had lived in Germany for hundreds of years, and Hugo told his wife Ruth there was no reason to worry about the Nazis. All their ranting and anti-Semitism was directed against the Polish Jews and religious types congregating in the big cities like Berlin. He scoffed at the idea of leaving Germany. He changed his mind in the hospital, after being beaten senseless during the *Kristallnacht* pogrom of 1938. As soon as he recovered, Hugo Spiegel hurried to Belgium and found a Catholic family in Brussels, the Bloomes, who offered to take in his family. He secured false documents for Ruth, nine-year-old daughter Rosa and infant son Paul. He returned home, saw that they got off safely, then planned to follow close behind. Too late. While he was desperately trying to reach Brussels during the German invasion in 1940, Hugo Spiegel was picked up by the SS, shipped off to Görs and later to the camps in the east. Distraught at losing her husband, Ruth Spiegel told her daughter to never speak German again in Nazi-occupied Brussels, especially to anyone wearing a uniform. But one day, a cheerful man wearing a suit approached Rosa on the school playground and began speaking with her in German. When she responded, he packed her into his car, screaming.

Ruth Spiegel grabbed her son and took the first train into the Belgian countryside. Trying her best to suppress a blind panic, she approached a Catholic family in the farm village of Chapelle la Herliemont and asked if they would take her son, then barely three years old. They said yes. She trusted them. Ruth Spiegel returned to Brussels and prayed that he at least would survive. She held her breath. Weeks turned into months, months became years. She worked as a scrubwoman and went through the war undetected, living with the Bloomes the entire time. Paul was raised as a "cousin from Germany" and learned French as his mother tongue.

His mother only dared to come see him once a year. His French was perfect. He carried a rosary. The family, and the village priest, however, never thought of converting the child. The rosary was his protection, they told her. In autumn 1944, with much of the country liberated by the British and Americans, Ruth Spiegel returned to Chapelle la Herliemont, thanked the family who had risked their lives protecting her son, and took him back to Brussels. As the Allies rolled westward into Germany, she waited and hoped to hear news that her daughter and husband might have survived. But by May 1945, she made plans to leave for America, where both she and Hugo Spiegel had family. With less than a week before departure, she received word that a man weighing less than 75 pounds had stumbled into Wahrendorf, asking if anyone had seen his wife, Ruth Spiegel. She tore up her American visa and headed home. She would never learn of Rosa's fate, save word from someone who thought they saw her, starved and emaciated, dying alone in Bergen-Belsen.

"My father never thought twice about where he would go after liberation," said an elegantly dressed Paul Spiegel one May morning 1996. We spoke in his Düsseldorf office, where he acts as an impresario and booking agent for musical acts. "My father said he hitch-hiked his way home to Wahrendorf and when he arrived, an old friend showed him that all the Hebrew books from the synagogue, the ones that hadn't been burned on *Kristallnacht*, had been kept safely in his basement during the war. Apparently, this meant something to him, and he was determined to start life over right there in Wahrendorf. He said he was too old to start in another country. As far as I know, he never even seriously considered leaving.

"Me, I was very young when we came home – eight years old. And I was panicked about being in Germany. After all, I had only heard they were murderers and horrible people. When I arrived with my mother, I refused to go to school and just stayed in my room. My father had a policeman come to the house and he said, 'So you're the Spiegel boy who refuses to go to school? Well, you've got to go.' I was so scared I went and on my very first day, someone in the class called me a dirty Jew. We got into a huge fight and it was pretty bloody. But I stood my ground and no one called me a name again.

"Right after that, my father was standing at the railroad yard loading cattle, and someone tried that with him – some anti-Semitic slur. A wrong move on that man's part. My father took his big walking stick and beat him bloody until people pulled him off and dragged them both to the British garrison commander. The officer behind the desk listened to the story, then shook his head. He looked at both of them and said, 'I have one question, Mr Spiegel. Why the hell didn't you finish the job?' And from that moment on, Freddie Berger became one of our family's closest friends. As it turned out, he was Jewish, and our house became the center for holidays and meals for all the Jewish soldiers in town. From that time on, he was uncle Freddie to me."

With no other Jews in Wahrendorf itself, Hugo Spiegel joined the Jewish community of Münster, where he served as vice president. At first there were only thirty Jews, but by the early 1950s, nearly one hundred and fifty had settled in the area. In 1951, Paul had the first bar mitzvah in North Rhine-Westphalia after the war.

Hugo Spiegel may have been well-known and respected in Wahrendorf but he and his wife quietly fretted about the fate of their son. A bar mitzvah was one thing, but there were almost no Jews for him to associate with. In 1955, he suggested that Paul might want to go to the summer camp run by ZWST (the Zentralwohlfahrtsstelle der Juden in Deutschland – the Central Welfare Agency of the Jews in Germany).

"I didn't want to go. I was petrified. 'Everyone will be super religious,' I told my father. 'Everyone will know everything about being Jewish – and I don't know anything, anything at all.' I can only imagine how much it must have hurt him to hear it." In the end Paul relented and took a train down to Frankfurt. Two weeks later, Paul Spiegel returned to Wahrendorf a different person. "What a shock! I had spent ten days with people just like me, and I really mean just like me. We had all the same stories, the same questions of identity, the same problems, the same fears bottled up inside. Suddenly, just like that, nothing was bottled up. I was a Jew, and I felt it."

And just as suddenly, Paul Spiegel couldn't bear staying in Wahrendorf. While he impatiently finished high school he managed to organize a Jewish youth club in nearby Münster. But as soon as he could, he packed his bags and moved to Düsseldorf. He began dating Giselle Spatz while working there at the Jewish newspaper. The two made plans to marry. A few weeks before the wedding, Paul Spiegel packed a small suitcase, threw it into his tiny Fiat 500, and puttered off westward, alone. He crossed the Belgian frontier and, pulling an address from his pocket, went to the apartment in Brussels of the Bloomes. He personally invited the elderly couple to his wedding. Then he asked them to help him locate the family who had saved his life. Digging through papers, the Bloomes provided Paul with a frayed photograph of him with the family and showed him on a map where they lived. He headed off to Chapelle la Herliemont, but no one in the tiny farming community said they had ever heard of the family. Concerned, thinking maybe they had lived out in the countryside, he traveled to nearby villages and knocked on doors, went into post offices, but always the same. No one could, or would, tell him a thing.

"So you know what I have to remember this family by?" he asked. He rolled up a pants leg to reveal a slight scar on his knee. "I remember one morning they took me to the door and said, 'Look, Paul, your mama is here,' and I saw her and I ran across the – what? the yard, the street – I'm not sure. But as I ran to her, I fell and cut my knee. So this scar is all I have." He rolled his pants leg down again. "My wife sometimes tells me I should try once more, I should go back, but I can't. It was painful thirty years ago not to find them. It would be worse now. You can't visit a dream. I tried, and I failed."

After his wedding, where the elderly Bloomes wiped away tears and smiled, after his honeymoon in London where uncle Freddie regaled the new bride with stories of how her young husband, when he was only so big, was like a mascot to the British garrison, Paul Spiegel went home to Düsseldorf and raised a family of his own. He has two daughters, one in Israel, the other in Frankfurt. Over the years, he became more and more involved with the Düsseldorf Jewish community as well as national Jewish institutions and went on to become president of ZWST. In the early 1960s, he worked with the next generation of youth in the Düsseldorf Jewish community center. One of the young people he worked with was Moshe Waks.

Waks, like the great percentage of Jews who settled in Germany after the war, did not come from German Jewish families like the Spiegels, but from East European stock. His father, Aron, was born in Lodz and spent the war years on the run in the Soviet Union, as did his mother, Leah Fleishmann. In 1945, the two met in Poland and decided to head to France together, but with no real papers, they were turned back at the border and ended up in a Displaced Persons camp in Kassel. Aron went to work for the Americans, saved his money and bought enough furniture and linens and goods to furnish an entire house. With an eye toward the exit, they shipped it all to Israel and planned to follow. Somehow, everything was stolen en route. They would have had nothing if they moved. Heartbroken, they decided to wait. Aron and Leah, with their sons Ruven, born in 1947, and Moshe, born five years later, moved to Düsseldorf. They opened a small clothing store.

"We spoke Yiddish at home, had our kosher food sent up from Frankfurt, and celebrated Shabbat every Friday by going to shul together," said Moshe Waks, a heavy set, cheerful man with a thick mustache. He now lives in Berlin and works in real estate and we spoke in his office there one January night in 1996. Moshe Waks said that when he was growing up in Düsseldorf, three days a week, after school, he and some thirty other youngsters gathered in the Jewish community center. A teacher traveled up from Essen to give Hebrew lessons and when he didn't come they studied about holidays and practiced the plays they would put on

Margot Rösler and her granddaughter in Berlin's Weissensee Jewish cemetery. The Rösler family fled Germany for Chile in the 1930s and return only to visit family graves. May 1995.

for their parents. Moshe's contacts with other Jewish children expanded at the ZWST summer camp.

What became clear in talking with Moshe Waks is that his childhood seemed as "normal" as any baby-boom-era Jewish childhood in the world. Even if it was in post-war Germany, when Düsseldorf had less than fifteen hundred Jews and the synagogue, burnt to the ground by neighbors, was still a pile of rubble. "I just never had a problem identifying myself as Jewish," he said with a shrug. "It started, I suppose, with my name. The other kids always asked what kind of name is that and I'd tell them. So I always had Jewish friends and non-Jewish friends.

"Now obviously, you begin to learn early that life as a Jew in Germany is different. Like whenever my father got angry, got a speeding ticket or something like that, he would explode and yell about the Nazis and the shocked policemen would always back down. But one day, when my father started calling this one young man a Nazi, the guy got so upset he just walked away. Two days later, the door rang and there he was at our house. My father couldn't believe it. 'What do you want?' he barked. And this guy, he said, 'Look Mr Waks, you got the wrong impression of me and my work and I came here just to explain that and clear things up with you.' Well, my father couldn't believe it. He got flustered and admitted he had done this only as a tactic, that he didn't even mean it. And then, standing there, he suddenly invited this young policeman into our home. He came in, my mother served coffee, everyone chatted, and that was the beginning of a very odd friendship – Aron Waks and Leon the policeman. Leon often came around to see him and talk about sports and he always brought his big German shepherd so I could play with him." Moshe Waks smiled. "As they say, go figure."

Still, as I learned in interview after interview with Jews born after the war, at some point, usually around the age of sixteen or so, each comes to realize that living in Germany is more than simply different. "When other Jewish kids from Belgium, Holland, or the US asked, 'Why are you in Germany?'" Waks said, "I would get defensive and give a standard Zionist reply. The Diaspora is all the same, I would tell them, so why pick on me? That's what I would say, but in my heart, I knew it was a jumbo problem to be a Jew in Germany."

It came as a mammoth jolt for Jewish youngsters after the war to understand that in their country, in their cities – perhaps in their very apartment buildings – men their fathers' or grandfathers' age rounded up Jews and massacred them, that women their mothers' or grandmothers' age watched as Jewish children were dragged out of their homes and shipped off to their deaths. Yet while beginning to understand what happened a few years before, they also ran into the hostility of their fellow-Jews from other lands. For many Jews in Germany, the only option was to flee.

Moshe Waks and his brother joined the ZJD (*Zionistische Jugend Deutschland* – Zionist Youth of Germany), an organization with one goal: to get Germany's youth to Israel. "Ruven became more and more Zionist and by high school, he moved to Israel. And I was right behind him. By the time I was in high school I didn't want to stay here at all."

Moshe Waks moved to Israel in 1973. He remained for seven years, but like a great many Jews from western Europe, beginning life over in Israel in the 1970s proved too difficult. He returned to Germany in 1980 when ZWST offered him a job running the youth programs of the Berlin community. Later he went into real estate, but Waks continued to volunteer in several community organizations, especially ZWST. When I asked him whether or not he felt at home in Germany today, and why he came back in 1980, he grinned. "Let me put it this way," he said as he started packing up his briefcase. "Psychologists have conducted a certain test. You take two groups of people and divide them. Ask one to move squares around a piece of paper and tell them they'll get, say, $10 for it. You tell the other group to do the same, only you don't tell them they'll get any money. Naturally, the groups are kept separate. Later, you ask both groups – individually – this question: why did you move the pieces around like you did? Now the first group, they invariably say, because I got paid, and that's the end of it. But the second group, they'll think, they'll ponder, they'll think some more, they'll give you all sorts of complicated answers to try and explain why they did what they did." He pushed himself away from the desk and smiled. "You see, Jews in Germany – we're that second group. And we've been trying to figure out why we've been here ever since – well, ever since we've been here."

Gabriele Fenyes is not untypical of the first generation of Jews born after the war. Tall, thin and chicly dressed, she lives in Hamburg where for twenty years she has worked as an executive with the Axel Springer publishing group. Her mother, born in Slovakia, survived deportation and Auschwitz. She was transported to a work camp in Bremen and was finally liberated from Bergen-Belsen. Her father, a Budapest attorney who had been active in Hungary's Social Democratic Party before the war, had a wife and two teenage children. They were deported all together. When he was liberated from a work camp near Hannover, he went searching for his family in Bergen-Belsen, where they had last been seen. They had not survived. In Belsen he met Gabriele's mother and the two stateless Jews, alone in the world with no family to return to, went no further than the nearest large city, Hannover. They married and had two daughters. Gabriele's father went to work on Jewish restitution matters for the state; her mother brought up her children within the Jewish community. "Only the two of them never spoke of the past. That door was closed, and it would stay that way," said Gabriele.

Even if Hannover's community was tiny, comprised of less than one hundred Jews then, Gabriele said, "Our upbringing was totally Jewish and we grew up proud and self-assured. In 1960, my best friend, Gabi Fürst and I, had the first bar mitzvahs in Lower Saxony since the war. We went to summer camp and we had a youth group. Yet we fit in with all our neighbors – until, that is, I became a teenager. That's when Zionism really took hold of me."

With several other friends, Gabriele Fenyes left Germany for Israel in 1971, "to test the waters, to see if I could really live there." Like many of her Zionist friends, she couldn't. "It just wasn't for me," she said with a sigh. "It was so hard to live in Israel then, to move there and start a whole life over. And German is my language, my mother tongue." She shrugged. "I grew up here. I came back here."

Gabriele Fenyes settled in Hamburg. She is now president of the Jewish community, where some 2,000 Jews live, including nearly 1,000 from the former Soviet Union and one hundred fifty or so from Iran. She travels through the whole of Schleswig-Holstein, Germany's thinly populated northernmost state, where she lends support to fledgling Jewish communities and lectures on Jewish themes in schools and churches. "But one thing I don't know about is my own family's past," she told me one November over lunch in an elegant Hamburg restaurant. "Over the years I've stumbled upon incidents, like a man from Budapest who told me that my father had saved his life. You can't imagine how proud that made me feel, to know something so noble about him, something he would never have mentioned himself. And I've even gone back to Budapest to visit the old family plot in the Jewish cemetery and to stand before my father's house in Pest." She grimaced slightly. "I even went searching through the antiquariats in his old neighborhood – they were filled with old photographs of the people around there, and I would search and search – but what for?" she said, raising her eyebrows. "I'll never know. He died more than twenty years ago."

Nor did she learn anything from her mother. *Die Zeit* recently ran a lengthy article about the Bremen camp, which Gabriele took to her mother, hoping she might tell her something, but she refused to speak. "Finally I was able to get her to go, just last year, to the fiftieth anniversary of the liberation of Belsen, and on the bus, she held my hand and said to me, 'Now I'm going to tell you everything.' She started by saying what her mother was wearing the day they came to take them away, but that's as far as she could go. And she's never said a word about it since."

This was more than just a wall of silence. It was closer to a shroud. Nearly every child of Holocaust survivors in Germany told me how much their parents did to keep the past from encroaching upon their children's lives. When I told a childhood friend of Gabriele's in Frankfurt that I had almost never been invited into a Jewish home in Germany, she smiled patiently, stubbed a cigarette, and said, "Look, when my parents came here after the concentration camps, they bought a huge apartment, the same one they have now. The door to the hallway had frosted glass in it, and the first thing they did was put up big iron bars. This was at a time when you didn't even need to close your door, much less lock it, but this is what they did. Then they installed three sets of chains.

"Like a great many survivors, they almost never invited anyone into their home. These people, the Polish concentration camp survivors that made up this community, were nearly – and with only a few exceptions – all like that. They would meet their friends outside, but home was different.

"When I was a child growing up, I didn't bring friends home. Oh, I did for a while, but the tension was electric, it was too much. So I stopped and met them outside.

"Once in a great while my father came home with someone from synagogue. Some poor nebbish alone in Frankfurt. But that was rare, and usually only for Pesach, when you're supposed to invite a stranger home. And food, food was not to enjoy. Just to eat, to be gotten through. The mood inside these homes, you could say, was cold, alone, and nearly dead. Like the lives of those who lived in them."

It was now 1996 – more than fifty years after the end of the war and I wondered if the younger generation of Jews, those born in the 1970s, was seeing things differently.

Rabbi Michael Goldberger in an afternoon Hebrew class in Düsseldorf's Jewish community center. October 1995.

Leo Hirschfeld, who was bar mitzvahed in the Neue Synagoge in Berlin, revisits the building on its inauguration as the Centrum Judaicum Museum in May 1995. Hirschfeld escaped Germany in the late 1930s.

Oliver Weiss' father, Maximillian, came from Presov, in Slovakia, and he escaped deportation during the war by hiding. He married late in life and he and his wife left Czechoslovakia after the Soviet-led invasion of 1968. They settled in Frankfurt and Oliver was born in 1971.

As a child, Oliver had his own way of dealing with being a Jew in Germany. He hid it from everyone. "No one knew I was Jewish except my very best friend. When I was bar mitzvahed, I insisted it be in Israel, not Frankfurt. I refused to go to Jewish programs, I only occasionally went to services with my father. But one day in class – I was fifteen years old – we were talking about the Holocaust and my friend turned around and said, 'Ask Oliver, he knows about that, he's Jewish.' And everyone said, 'Hey, really?'"

"I was totally and completely shocked. I had been" – he chuckled, "outed. As a Jew. And I was not happy one bit." Oliver Weiss had spent his entire childhood – up until that moment – trying to avoid a crisis of identity he could see would be there if he let it out in public. His way of dealing with it was to deny it to the world. But this was no longer an option. He leaned back in his chair and smiled. "Yeah, outed."

A few months later, Oliver Weiss entered high school. Unlike his earlier school, there were Jewish kids in every grade, ten to fifteen in each, some sixty altogether. They hung around together, went for sodas after school, played sports, were clearly a clique. "And this is when I started making friends. Jewish friends. And it was, I must say, a natural bond. Oh, I used to hate going to the community center, but not any more. Suddenly I got involved with making a Jewish newspaper, which I did in high school and I'm still involved with one now. But in the midst of my becoming Jewish, openly Jewish, I watched as my father soured on Germany and grew to love Israel more and more. I began thinking, and it was logical, then, for me to go and explore Israel myself. After all, I had to find a way – and a place – to define my Jewishness. So while I was deeply involved with my Jewish friends in Frankfurt, as soon as high school was over I decided I would go and spend a summer in Israel. It was something of a test for me, to see if I could live there."

Oliver Weiss hoped that being in Israel would forge his identity. It did, but not in the way he had planned. Living on a kibbutz, he told an older kibbutznik he would be sure to stay in touch from Frankfurt. The man barked, "Don't! I don't even want a stamp in my house from that horrible place." And one day a young woman interrupted Oliver as they were chatting, and said, "Hey, what is it with you? You're such a Yekke! Can't you just stop thinking all the time? Can't you just do something and not think, think, think?"

Oliver Weiss smiled and shook his head. "I mean, she used the word think with such derision! Well I just looked at her, and that's when I realized, and I blurted out to this girl, 'Okay, so I'm German.' And that's when I knew I was never going to live in Israel, because that's how I see the world – as a German. Or, well, perhaps, as a European. But for a while at least, I'm staying here."

One Frankfurt Jewish family thought seriously of not staying. Annette Ackermann was one of three sisters born to two Holocaust survivors. During the worst months of neo-Nazi violence in 1991, she and her American-born husband Michael, an attorney, decided to leave Frankfurt for the United States. They discussed the issue with their three children and in the summer of 1992, moved to South Florida. Since they were financially well off, they chose the most highly recommended Jewish school in the region. Annette was nervous about how well her two school age boys would do. After all, neither had spent time in the United States and they learned their English at home and in Frankfurt schools. "Our oldest son, Aby, a senior, tested completely off the charts, so immediately we were a little concerned about how much good a US high school could do him." Worse to come was a series of depressing incidents "that made us feel as if we'd been dropped from another planet."

Aby, who was making straight A's from his first week, also led the school to its first ever soccer tournament. Yet he was subjected to endless needling from the teachers. "Are you circumcised?" asked one bluntly, apparently confusing him with the great majority of Jews from the former Soviet Union who are not. "Hey Berlin Wall!" another liked to chide him in front of the other students, finding this side-splittingly funny. The dean of the school asked Aby if Auschwitz was in Germany. One day he came home nearly blind with fury. "A teacher said they would be making a class trip to Washington, DC, and they'd be taking the bus up from Miami. Aby raised his hand and asked, since it was such a long distance, if taking the train was possible, which he hadn't yet done in America. The teacher sneered and said, 'Well, we all know about what happened to Jews on the trains in Germany, don't we?'" Annette rolled her eyes. "It really hurt me to see him having to go through this. I honestly never imagined we'd run into this kind of insensitivity – from Jews."

The younger son, Saly, aged nine, went home one day with another young boy. The boy's mother panicked to hear that "a German" was enrolled in the Jewish school, She phoned the director to discuss the matter. A few days later, the boy he had visited quietly took Saly aside and whispered, "Were there Nazis in your family?"

Annette Ackermann threw up her hands. "Now where do you suppose a nine year old would pick up that kind of talk?"

It seemed to her that ignorance and insensitivity were everywhere and inescapable. One night a real estate dealer came to the Ackermann home. He had said he wanted to talk with them about something important. Michael welcomed him in. Annette served coffee and cake. Gathered around the kitchen table, the realtor suggested that Michael and Annette work with him to try and find other German Jews who would soon be fleeing Germany for America as the Nazis were sure to be taking over again. If they would cooperate and help him sell some houses, he said with a smile, he'd be sure to cut them a deal. "All we could do was smile and thank him for his offer," Annette said.

Another Jewish neighbor sought Annette out to tell her she was glad the Ackermanns had come over to America – and just in time – but if the other Jews in Frankfurt or Berlin wanted to come and needed help, she would never give it, "because they decided to stay in Germany after the war," she told me.

The Jewish family that left Germany, in part, to get away from Germans, had found itself so thoroughly labeled as German that Annette and Michael thought it over and decided there was only one thing to do. In the summer of 1994, they returned to Frankfurt. "And since we've been back, I have to say that I feel more at home than ever. This is not to say every Jew doesn't have problems of identity here. That comes with the territory. But whether you call yourself a German Jew or a Jew in Germany or a Jew with German citizenship, it doesn't matter. There is Jewish life here, and we are part of it."

A World Rebuilt

Jewish life re-established itself in Germany after the war, despite the difficulties of being a Jew in the land of the perpetrator, despite pressure from the outside for Jewish life never again to be rekindled on German soil. In 1950, international Jewish organizations vowed not to recognize a Jewish community in the Federal Republic, but those who lived there formed the *Zentralrat der Juden in Deutschland* (Central Council of Jews in Germany), to look after political aspects of the various communities in the country. A year later the *Zentralrat* re-established ZWST, the *Zentralwohlfahrtsstelle der Juden in Deutschland* (Central Welfare Council of Jews in Germany), which had looked after the welfare needs of Jews throughout the country from 1914 until it was closed down by the Nazis. The titles make clear the Jews' own ambiguous position. These were not organizations of German Jews, but rather of Jews in Germany. And true enough, much of the Jewish life that was reconstructed after 1945 was the work of Jews who settled in Germany after the war, from Poland mainly, and later from Hungary and Czechoslovakia.

Munich Jewish community leaders at a commemoration service in the Dachau concentration camp.

Zuriel Tsah at the Jewish elementary school in Berlin at a Friday night Shabbat dinner for parents and children. March 1993.

Much of the rebuilding as well as the operational costs, were – and continue to be – underwritten by various state and local governments in Germany, not by Jews themselves. During the two decades following the war, everything from community life to relations with the authorities was carried out quietly, and as far from the public spotlight as possible. No one wanted a high profile. Jews claimed to be sitting on packed suitcases.

That started to change in the late 1960s. While young non-Jewish Germans began challenging their parents about the past, the first German-born Jews to reach university age were confronting what they described as the ghetto mentality of their parents. Since, as we have seen above, many could not identify with being German, more than a few left the country, heading to Israel and other countries to study, live and find work. They wanted to escape the burden of living as a Jew in Germany. But throughout the 1970s and early 1980s, many returned. Yet they would no longer accept the status quo – either at home or from their neighbors.

Two events in Frankfurt in the 1980s signaled a turning point in Jewish consciousness in Germany. On October 31, 1985, thirty Jews – real estate developers, intellectuals, housewives, students – walked onto the stage of the Frankfurt *Schauspielhaus* before the premier performance of Rainer Werner Fassbinder's "Garbage, the City and Death" and prevented the play – which featured an insatiably greedy Jewish real estate speculator – from being performed. They accused it of being openly anti-Semitic. Sitting on the edge of the stage, this curious gathering of Jews engaged the audience in discussion about why they felt compelled to protest. Later they gave interviews to newspapers and were seen and heard on television and radio. A line had been crossed. Jews – actual living Jews – were out of Germany's closet.

A year later, in 1986, a new Jewish community center in Frankfurt opened its doors. The difference between it and its Berlin counterpart speaks volumes. One, a drab building of featureless, cold stone, was built in 1959 to administer a tiny and dispirited community. The other, opened three decades later, was filled with classrooms, lounges, youth clubs and playgrounds. They are both reflections of the time they were built. (Berlin's community services are now housed in a minimum of four separate buildings servicing the largest community in the country: 10,200. Frankfurt's now stands at 6,000 plus.) "From the day we opened this building," said Frankfurt Jewish community center director Stefan Szajak, "we unpacked the proverbial suitcases that Jews here were supposedly sitting on. It was a major psychological move."

This new awakening was followed by three events that put Jews back on their guard. The first was German unification itself. It was not the thought of living with eighty million Germans – after all, what is the difference between the sixty plus million of the Federal Republic plus those from the former East? It was the fear of creating a too-powerful, too-dominant Germany within Europe. We all know what happened the last time Germany was Europe's most powerful state.

Jews in Germany gritted their teeth, there was a sharp intake of breath, followed by the fervent wish that a big Germany would remain as democratic as the Federal Republic had been.

Almost immediately, however, a wave of anti-foreigner and neo-Nazi violence rocked the country. A black man was murdered on a train in Brandenburg. Skinheads torched apartments for asylum seekers in eastern German cities of Rostock

and Hoyerswerda while neighbors gathered to cheer. Vandals set fire to the Jewish barracks at the Sachsenhausen concentration camp. West Germans hurried to point out that all this new violence was taking place in the former East Germany. But then in the west, a man merely thought to be a Jew was killed near the Dutch border (he wasn't Jewish). Turkish families were burned to death in arson attacks in Mölln and Solingen. Jewish cemeteries were defaced in several cities and the Lübeck synagogue was fire bombed.

The *Zentralrat*, which had always received anonymous hate mail, noticed the letters were now being signed. The mayor of a village not far from Mainz wrote to tell the *Zentralrat* how glad he was no Jew lived in his town. Was all this a harbinger of worse to come? Voices were raised criticizing the German justice systems for being too tepid in the sentences it meted out to murderers and thugs.

The third event was the Gulf War. While Israelis stared at each other through gas masks, German mothers claimed to be afraid and bought out whole grocery stores. While Hans Christian Ströbele, spokesman of the Green party, said, "The Iraqi missile attacks on Israel are the logical, almost unavoidable outcome of Israel's policies," Edna Brocke, director of the Jewish Museum in Essen, watched as the Jewish-Christian friendship society she had been a member of broke up amid bitter recriminations. "I had to ask myself, had we ever been talking the same language? Had all those years been in vain?"

These developments shocked, disturbed and worried Jews. What was different now, however, was that they raised their voices openly and aired their concerns. From officials such as Heinz Galinski, president of the *Zentralrat*, to writers and essayists like Julius Schoeps, Ralf Giordorno, Dan Diner, Micha Brumlik and especially Henryk Broder, Jews went on television and radio and churned out scores of articles for the bestknown newspapers and magazines in the country. They let their point be known: that German anti-war behavior during the Gulf War was – for the most part – a disguise for anti-Israelism.

During the Gulf War and afterwards, Ignatz Bubis, who became president of the *Zentralrat* after Galinski died in 1992, seemed to be everywhere, taking on a public persona that was unprecedented for a post-war Jewish leader. Working the halls of the *Bundestag*, giving interviews, talking to school groups and universities, opening exhibitions, the man became a staple fixture of public life in Germany. Bubis never shied away from insensitive or provocative questions, and he was forthright and candid in his replies. Yet he nearly always injected just enough irony to lighten the situation, and by 1996 he had become one of Germany's most effective diplomats. His portfolio, it seemed to me, was to explain Germans to themselves. There was even a brief movement in 1994 to draft him for President of Germany. He declined the offer with a bemused chuckle, though he maintained an active role in the Free Democratic Party, both nationally as well as at home in Frankfurt. He was one of several Jews to take up mainstream political activism, and Bubis' second in command at the *Zentralrat*, Frankfurt lawyer Michel Friedman, is on the national board of Chancellor Kohl's Christian Democrats while social worker Peter Feldmann is a Frankfurt representative of the Social Democrats.

The post-war Hannover synagogue. August 1992.

The vast majority of Jews, however, do not engage in public forums. Many actively participate in Jewish community functions, and Frankfurt community center director Stefan Szajak walked me through the programs they carry out. "Before the recent influx of Jews from the Soviet Union," he said, "we were an older community. Now the average age of our 6,000 Jews is around forty-three. We have the very old and we have young families now, but it's the in-between generations where we're weak. Our numbers rise only by those who arrive."

Caring for the elderly in a community like Frankfurt's is especially difficult, he said. Many of the old, who do not receive full pensions and whose reparation payments do not quite support them, are given financial aid by the Jewish community and ZWST. The Jewish old age home has two hundred-seven residents. "But a lot of people want to stay at home, and we have to respect that."

"Our kosher restaurant makes lunch every day, and we send our driver around for the infirm," Szajak went on. "A few years ago, we started getting non-Jewish volunteers who chose civil service over the army. We send them around to clean apartments and do the shopping. We have Jewish social workers on staff who visit people at home every week, and three full-time nurses make the rounds and report back to us. The social workers do whatever they can to pull the people out of their shells. We want them to come here, play cards, listen to concerts, go on trips. Much of this we do in conjunction with ZWST, which now runs a resort hotel in Bad Kissingen. It's a great thing to be able to send the old people off for a week in the Black Forest, to be in a Jewish environment, stay with friends, have kosher food."

Sitting in Szajak's fourth floor office, we could hear the sound of children at play below. Across the courtyard is the kindergarten, with one hundred-twenty children, and the elementary school, with three hundred students. It was recess time. I went over to the window to watch children playing, chasing each other, jumping rope. Szajak cocked his head slightly and smiled. "It's the best thing about this community center. It really lives. And our happiest problem is that the school has really outgrown us."

From the time I signed up as a member of the

Afternoon at the Jewish community center in Frankfurt/Main.
March 1996.

Ignatz Bubis, chairman of the Central Council of Jews in Germany,
attending a session of the Bundestag. November 1993.

Berlin Jewish community in 1992 until 1996, the
number of Jews grew from 9,200 to 10,200. A drop
in the bucket compared to the 170,000 pre-war, but
one does not build a community by focusing back-
wards. With that in mind, Jews in Berlin, Frankfurt
and Munich opened kindergartens in the early
1970s and by the 1980s they started jewish-run elementary schools as well.

Now there is even a newly-opened high school
in Berlin and by 1995, with five hundred Berlin
children in community schools, the first newly-con-
structed Jewish elementary school on German soil
since the war was opened. The community held an

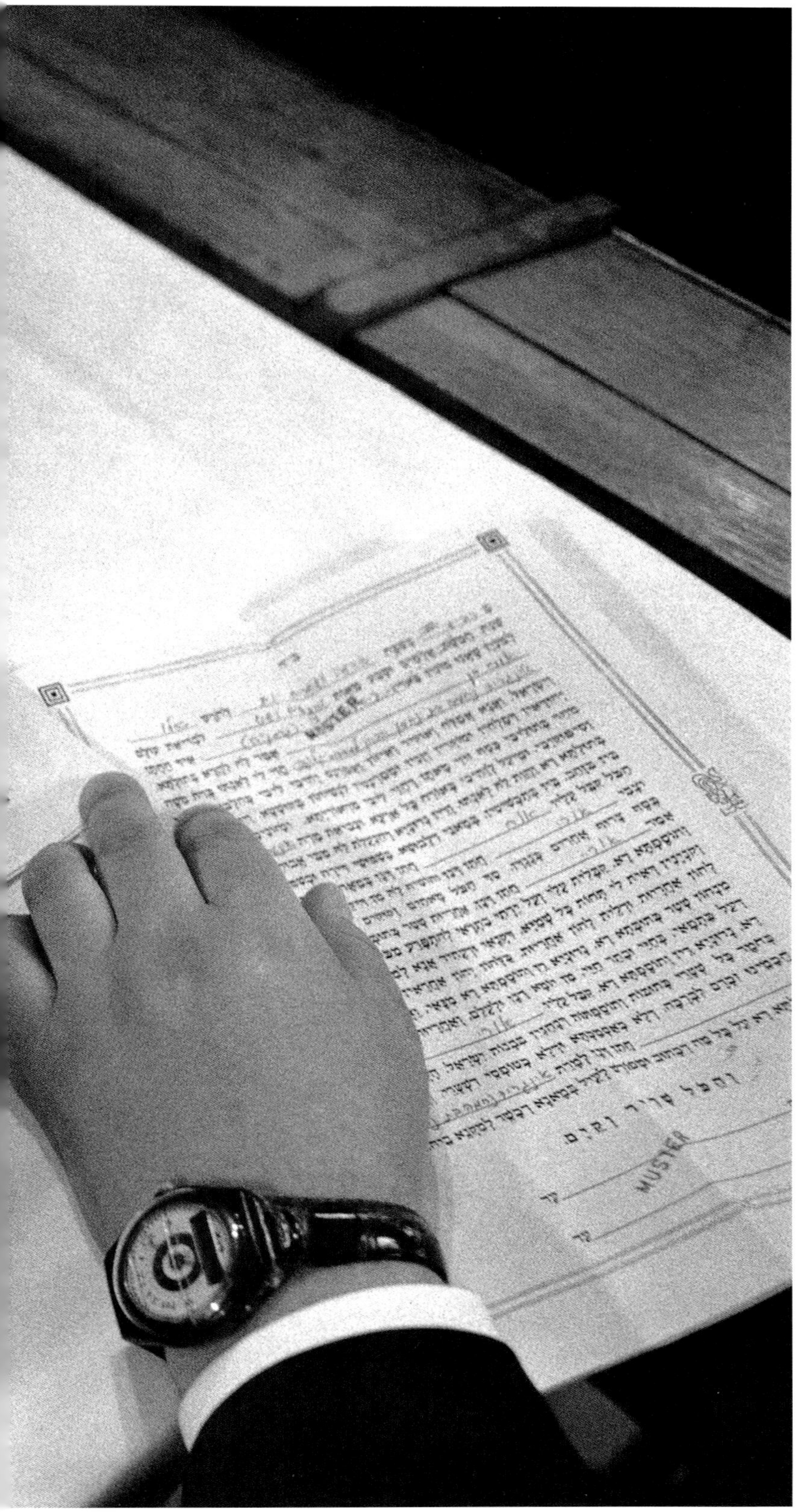

Wedding ceremony of Juri Brener and Ingrid Klueger in the Düsseldorf synagogue. October 1995.

Rabbi Gochwald signing the wedding certificate of Juri Brener and Ingrid Klueger in the Düsseldorf synagogue. October 1995.

architectural competition for the new campus, which drew eighty-three submissions. The designs were judged anonymously – and an Israeli, Zvi Hecker, won both the job and several subsequent architectural awards. With white curved walls arching around in elegant wings that look like giant sails, the building is constructed of stucco, wood and corrugated metal. While other Jewish institutions throughout Europe often look like armed fortresses, here are open terraces, huge shade trees whith circular benches ringing them, and everywhere, Hecker's looming walls that sail and swoop.

Maccabia sports games, Berlin. July 1992.

Miki wastes not. ZWST summer camp in Sobernheim. August 1992.

Just after lunch at Sobernheim, Arthur and friends take to their chair in song. August 1992.

Inside, the hallways move in S-shaped curves that seem to invite the children to run through them. An obviously pleased German president, Roman Herzog, attended the opening of the school, and standing next to him was a beaming Norma Drimmer, the community's educational representative.

Drimmer, whose own parents had lived through the concentration camps and was educated in the Sorbonne in Paris, is passionate about the school and wholly dedicated to it. Meeting me one day at the entrance to walk me through Hecker's complex design, she told me something chilling. "Remember, this school cost fifteen percent more than any other school to build. We stayed completely within the framework that the Berlin senate laid out for all schools. The additional costs were for what there had to be – security. Bullet proof doors and windows on the ground floor, special alarms, gates and walls."

Two hundred-forty students were enrolled in 1996, taught by eighty teachers, including a dozen from Israel. "I remember how nervous we were back in 1986 when we opened our first school," Drimmer said. "We had only twenty-five students and I never thought it would get to be much bigger." She looked at the scores of children bustling noisily through the halls, smiled, and rolled her eyes. "Well, when we built this school, we made sure it could accomodate four hundred students. And I think, I really think, it won't need to be bigger than that." She smiled like a cheshire cat. "I mean, can you imagine? Ten years ago twenty-five students, now two hundred-fifty?"

I thought about the new school and the new generation of children it served when I visited the Moses Mendelssohn high school in former East Berlin. The school had been closed by the Nazis; during the Communist period it had been used as a trade school. The Berlin Jewish community was given back the property in 1991 and it re-opened the school in 1993. By 1996 the student body topped two hundred. Watching from a third floor window, I looked down at the playground. Kids were chatting, chasing each other around. To me it was an illustration of a Jewish future. From my vantage point, though, I could see something else. Just on the other side of the high stone wall that marked the

edge of the playground was the old Grosse Hamburger Strasse Jewish cemetery, where Moses Mendelssohn's tomb is the only one still standing. Tourists gathered in a circle around Mendelssohn's grave to listen to a lecture about the Jewish past. I shifted my gaze to back toward the Jewish future.

The Mendelssohn school is part of a neighborhood whose Jewish presence is ever more apparent. Around the corner is the Centrum Judaicum, a Jewish museum recently opened in the newly reconstructed Oranienburger Strasse synagogue, the city's largest and most splendid before the war. The synagogue was only partially destroyed on *Kristallnacht*, thanks to the heroism of a non-Jewish policeman who chased the Nazis away and summoned the fire wagons. But later it was seriously damaged by Allied bombs, and the wrecked sanctuary, whose windows once upon a time were kept frost free in the winter with tiny gas jets, was eventually toppled by cranes in the 1960s. The rest of the building, its once-magnificent dome collapsed in a heap, remained as a brooding skeleton with bushes and even trees growing out of the rubble.

In 1988, the East German government announced the building would be restored – except for the sanctuary – and turned into a Jewish Museum. Hermann Simon, an East German Jewish historian, was asked to be its director. He and I spoke several times in 1988 an 1989. I pegged him for a cold aparatchik. But after the Wall fell and East Germany collapsed, Simon stubbornly kept championing his museum and much to his, and the Berlin senate's credit, construction never stopped. Simon became easier going and more cheerful. By 1994, as the synagogue's gold dome was restored, he even started telling jokes. It was a solemn-faced Hermann Simon though, who, in May 1995, accompanied the President and Chancellor of Germany to the museum's opening on the fiftieth anniversary of the end of the war in Europe. In its first year, the Centrum Judaicum saw over 180,000 visitors.

This part of Berlin, the old Spandauer Vorstadt, shows the diversity and vibrancy of Jewish life better than anywhere else in Germany. All around, Jewish groups are trying to forge their own iden-

Purim parade on Oranienburger Strasse in Berlin, March 1994.

Jonas Melchers and Phillip Kein before Shabbat services in Berlin's Pestalozzi Strasse synagogue. March 1993.

tities. The first time I met Simon, he was vice president of the one hundred-ninety member East Berlin community, which had exactly half the total registered Jewish population of the East German state. Since reunification, he had become a member of the West Berlin community, which took over the property and programs of the now defunct eastern community. But a few East Berlin Jews chose not to join the unified community and started their own Jewish Cultural Society, which opened a

few doors down the street from the Centrum Judaicum. Since it did not have its own synagogue, permanent teacher or rabbi, its Jewish content may not have been all that strong, but it genuinely met the needs of those Jews who felt the larger community was not addressing their concerns. Its chairperson was the fiesty Irene Runge. Ever on the attack in manner of the communist-style polemicist, Runge was giving Jews a place to congregate and be together. Around the corner, Mario Offenburg, whose father had led a small orthodox Jewish community in Berlin before the war, is trying to do the same in and around his small synagogue, which also has a strictly kosher restaurant and kosher

Page 106/107
Rabbi Ernst Stein gives Jonas Melchers a sip of wine during the Purim festival service in Berlin's Pestalozzi Strasse synagogue. March 1993.

Amalie Strauch at Janette Wolf Old Age Home in Berlin. November 1992.

food shop attached to it. Throughout Germany, in fact diversity is rearing its head, a concept not altogether welcomed by the *Zentralrat*.

Until recently, post-war religious life in Germany was completely in the hands of orthodox Jews, despite the fact that very few Jews in Germany would define themselves as orthodox. And while members of the *Zentralrat* complained they had great difficulty in finding orthodox rabbis who would come to Germany, their constituency was obviously crying out for liberalization. When the tiny Jewish communities of Oldenburg and Braunschweig hired a woman rabbi in 1995, the *Zentralrat* sharply stated its opposition to the move.

This was somewhat ironic, as Germany, after all, had its first woman rabbi in the 1930s. When several Frankfurt Jews started their own liberal congregation in 1994, the *Zentralrat* was no more enthusiastic. This too was ironic, given Germany's historic role as the cradle of reform Judaism.

With the continuing influx of Jews from the former Soviet Union, things will change in Germany's Jewish communities. Just as the *Zentralrat* was dominated by Jews who came from Polish Jewish stock, in time, Jews from even further east will take their place. They already make up the majority of members in many communities throughout the country.

Former East German spymaster Markus Wolf with Israel's first consul general to Berlin, Mordechai Levi, at a Hanukkah party in the Jewish Cultural Association. December 1994.

Prof. Dr. Rita Süssmuth, President of the Bundestag, at a reception in her honor in the Düsseldorf Jewish community center. October 1995.

Commemoration service at the Buchenwald concentration camp. May 1995.

Dani Levi showing off her Very Good grades in the Itzhak Rabin School in Düsseldorf. October 1995.

Excercise class in the Jewish elementary school, Berlin. December 1994.

Tatmittelmeldedienst für Spreng- und Brandvorrichtungen

BKA

Hinweise zum Erkennen von Brief- und Paketbomben

Jeder kann Opfer einer »Brief- oder Paketbombe« werden, da sowohl im allgemeinkriminellen als auch im terroristischen Bereich diese Sprengvorrichtungen immer wieder dazu benutzt werden, Personen gezielt anzugreifen.

Die nachfolgenden Punkte sollen als *Hilfestellung* für das Erkennen von »Brief- und Paketbomben« dienen, sie dürfen jedoch *nicht* als *abschließende Aufzählung* verstanden werden.

- *Wahrscheinlichkeit, als Opfer in Frage zu kommen (z. B. vorausgegangene Drohung, politische Tätigkeit, ausländische Staatsangehörigkeit usw.)*

- *Post aus dem Ausland, Luftpost oder Auslieferung durch private Paketzustelldienste oder erkennbar nicht durch Post zugestellt (ohne Briefmarken, kein Poststempel usw.)*

- *Unbekannter Absender oder fehlender Absender*

- *Hinweise auf dem Umschlag, wie »Vertraulich«, »Privat«, »Persönlich« usw.*

- *Handgeschriebene oder schlecht leserliche Adressen*

- *Adresse steht nicht am üblichen Platz*

- *Unkorrekte Titel oder Dienstgrade*

- *Angabe eines Titels, aber keine Namensangabe*

- *Auffallende Rechtschreibfehler*

- *Postsendung ist über das notwendige Maß frankiert*

- *Ölige Flecken oder Verfärbungen, herausragende Drähte oder Metallfolie*

- *Ungewöhnlich hohes Gewicht der Postsendung in Bezug auf ihr Format*

- *Fester Umschlag oder ungewöhnlich stabile Verpackung*

- *Unebener Umschlag bzw. fühlbare Gegenstände im Innern des Umschlages*

- *Übertriebene Versiegelung der Postsendung/Sicherung mit Klebeband und Schnur*

Student being interviewed by reporters on the opening day of the
Grosse Hamburger Strasse high school in August 1994.

Jerzy Kanal, president of the Berlin Jewish community, discussing the
opening of the first Jewish high school in Germany since the Third Reich.
August 1993.

Page 114/115: Child's Hanukkah drawing and bomb-threat instructions
on a wall in the Berlin Jewish elementary school. March 1995.

Reception at the Israeli Consulate in honour of a Berlin resident who
hid Jews during World War II. May 1993.

Jewish policemen from New York City at the opening of the
Centrum Judaicum, Berlin, May 1995. The building was once a
synagogue. When Nazis tried to burn the building on Kristallnacht, a
non-Jewish policeman stopped them. 57 years later, these Jewish
policemen came to pay their respects.

The Russians are Coming

One afternoon in the spring of 1990, Mary Sofer, an Israeli who had been living in Germany for nearly twenty years, was just closing the office of the Jewish Council of Lower Saxony in Hannover when the telephone rang. "It was a friend of mine who said a Russian Jewish man had just arrived in Hannover and he wanted to live here. She wanted to know if I could help." So Mary Sofer drove over to meet the man, took down some information, then set about making phone calls to city offices where she could obtain permission for him to live in Hannover, plus medical insurance, a language course, an apartment, social welfare help. "It took two full days of phone calls and visits and letter writing, but I did it. And just as I finished putting everything into a file, the telephone rang again. It was another Russian. This time a family. They had just arrived. They wanted to live here. They needed help." She smiled broadly. "You know, sometimes I wish I hadn't picked up the phone that first time."

One of the strange side effects of the fall of the Berlin Wall and the collapse of the Soviet Union is the fact that Jewish life in Germany – or at least its Jewish population – has been revived. In 1990 there were 28,000 registered Jews in Germany. Since then 25,000 immigrants have entered community logbooks. In city after city, they have exploded the numbers. Hannover's three hundred-eighty Jews now have over twelve hundred new Jewish neighbors.

Düsseldorf's community shot up from 2,000 to 3,500 in five years. Berlin, which has been ac-

cepting Jews from the east since Cold War Detente days, has around 3,500 original post-war residents – plus twice that many Russians, White Russians, Georgians, Ukraines, Latvians, Lithuanians, Estonians, Khazaks, etc. And in the former East Germany, whole new communities have sprung up, created by the new immigrants.

In every way possible, these new arrivals have overwhelmed the communities and are taxing their social welfare and educational systems to the limit. They are also giving the aging and insular Jewish communites of Germany something they had not had until now: a real future.

The problem of integrating thousands into communities of hundreds is daunting enough. ZWST has thrown itself into coordinating the process. With its headquarters in Frankfurt, ZWST professionals travel the country to meet with city administrators in order to secure decent housing and language lessons for the new immigrants, while ZWST teachers instruct the ex-Soviet citizens in basic lessons about Jewish tradition and lore. There is much to be taught: former citizens of the ex-Soviet Union know almost nothing of Judaism after being afraid to practice their religion for generations. Not all of them wish to become re-acquainted with their Judaism however, and many are more concerned with learning a new language and figuring out how to cope in a competitive, capitalist society.

To help integrate those who are interested, ZWST offers weekends at Bad Kissingen, a resort hotel in the Black Forest, and the Sobernheim all-year camp. Weekends are set aside solely for mothers and their children to come and learn Jewish customs, cooking, singing. Other seminars

Jewish youth from the ex-Soviet Union on their way to their first ZWST summer camp in Sobernheim.

are strictly job-oriented – four day seminars where artists meet art directors, designers and magazine editors, or where musicians get a chance to discuss matters with record company executives, booking agents and restaurant owners.

In November 1995, I rode a local regional train from Frankfurt to Sobernheim in order to observe a musicians seminar. From the tiny station, the Jewish camp was a short car ride away, tucked into the hills of the scenic Rhineland, and I could hear the sound of violinists practicing from the second and third floor windows as soon as I arrived. While an Israeli cook was preparing dinner in a nearby kitchen, twenty-six musicians were listening to a lecture in the social hall by the retired director of the Frankfurt Academy of Music. He discussed the need for proper résumés and explained that follow-up calls had to be made after sending them off. He held up examples of the various professional publications and showed which ones had the best classified ads.

After the lecture, as people drifted off or cornered the professor, Elena Dragiewa sat shaking her head. "I've been in Germany a year," she said sadly, "and all I do is crank out letters and sample tapes. I've gotten absolutely nowhere."

Elena Dragiewa came from Riga where she had lived with her husband and son. She taught piano and accompanied opera singers at their recitals in Riga and elsewhere and had been working steadily for nearly three decades. But after 1989, as Latvia moved toward independence, she and her family, who spoke no Latvian, lost most of their freelance jobs. "They told us, 'go back to Russia'. But we're not Russian! I just speak the language and I sure don't want to go there." By the time they were earning a mere fifty lat per month, "when you need one hundred just to eat," she and the family applied to come to Germany.

"Now we live in a one room flat in a crowded barracks with seven hundred other people in an East German village called Aschwara. That I can put up with. But I'm desperate to work and as I said, I send out letters all the time." She wrung her hands. Looking at me imploringly, she said, "I must work. I always work. And yesterday, another man was here from Frankfurt, from a music school. So I ran up to my room and I gave him my papers." She

started wringing her hands again. "Maybe, maybe..." Her son Dmitri came up and sat beside her.

"But I'm sure we made the right choice," she said looking at him, half trying to convince herself in the process.

Later, Marian Perlmutter, who ran the program for the Russian musicians, sighed and said that Elena Dragiewa was taking matters hard. With each rejection her blood pressure climbed so high she had been hospitalized twice. "I hope things get better for her," Perlmutter said, "but you know, a good eighty percent of new Russian immigrants – and some have been here five years or more – haven't found jobs." He winced. "Well," and his eyes scanned the room. "At least for the musicians, things can be a bit easier. Not easy. But easier."

Igor Epstein, a stocky Lithuanian-born violinist with dancing eyebrows and wearing a leather vest, hadn't wasted his time mailing anything to anyone. As we sat talking in his rom upstairs at Sobernheim after dinner, he said, "I came to Cologne four years ago and just went knocking on doors. I'm a damned good violinist but I spent quite a few nights eating boiled noodles and ketchup and earning all of ten marks for a whole evening of playing to a handful of drunks. Now I'm eating better," – he patted his not inconsiderable girth – "and earning four hundred marks per hour in some really fine places." He handed me a handsomely printed color brochure with his face beaming on the cover, violin tucked under his chin. On the back was written, "References: Hotel Kempinski, Hyatt Regency, the Chancellor's Ball, Le Ball Des Sports." Inside was a list of his awards and achievements. Holding his violin while we talked, he asked me where I was from. When I said Savannah, Georgia, he began playing "Orange Blossom Special." "But I moved to Hungary in 1988," I said. He slipped into a gypsy melody, and while he played, he asked, "and you're Jewish?" When I nodded, Igor set his violin squealing, "my Yiddische Mama" with all the schmaltz he could muster.

Music of another kind brought me to the freshly repainted synagogue in Leipzig in September 1995. The event was Rosh Hashanah, the somber beginning of the Jewish new year. I greeted Leo Adlerstein, the head of Leipzig's Jewish community.

Russian Jewish youths in the Berlin Jewish Youth Center. November 1995.

Things had changed since I had met him in 1988. Back then, he had had twenty-eight Jews under his care. Now the surrounding region was home to more hundreds than he wished to count. The state of Saxony (which also includes Dresden) was housing thousands of Russian Jewish immigrant families in tiny apartments, former East German army barracks, and, in some cases, decrepit, substandard housing. To alleviate conditions, ZWST arranged buses to fetch the far-flung Jewish families to bring them to Jewish communites in Leipzig, Erfurt and Dresden whenever they could, and particularly for holiday ceremonies and celebrations.

Adlerstein had aged poorly since I had seen him last in 1992. The elderly Buchenwald survivor looked ill and pallid but he slowly made his way up to the altar of the synagogue that September morning and began leading a service. Every seat was taken – I counted nearly two hundred souls. Almost every one of them was Russian, and I did not see one chant along with the service. There was not a prayer book in the entire room – in Hebrew, German or Russian. These people were, in fact, completely lost in a Jewish prayer service. Oddest of all, and something I never heard before during a synagogue service, was this: silence. Everyone was reverentially quiet and there was not a child in sight. In the Pestalozzi Strasse synagogue in Berlin, children usually crawl over the benches, gnaw at each others ankles, and take their mini-prayer shawls and race down the aisles pretending to be Superman. Even at the far more orthodox synagogue on Joachimstaler Strasse, Rabbi Weiss regularly pulls out what looked like an oversized mallet and whacks his tiny podium when the kibitzing gets too loud.

Standing in the back of the Leipzig sanctuary was a short man in a leather jacket. His name was Yossi Vardi, and it was upon his shoulders the entire Russian program for the old East German states lay. Born in western Russia, he and his family fled to China early in the war, first to Harbin, later to Shanghai. After the war they moved to Israel, and Yossi Vardi came to Berlin in 1991 to work for his old friend, Bennie Bloch, the director of ZWST. Known to be a tough administrator, Yossi had a large territory to cover, Jews scattered around in hundreds of locations, and old GDR communities that have not been overly helpful. He shook his head as if he had read my thoughts. "Look. So they're not so frum (orthodox)," he said in a hoarse whisper. "But at least we make them feel wanted, and most of them have never, not ever, been in a synagogue in their lives. We are dealing with people completely removed from their religion – and that is not going to change overnight."

Working with the Russians, Yossi – as he put it – was "building Jews." So was Monika Domaij-Gaul, a Jewish woman in Kassel who met me as I stepped off a gleaming white ICE express train in the Kassel station a couple of days after Rosh Hashanah. Smiling and slipping my camera bag into the back seat, she gunned her small Opel up the autobahn heading north, exited and cut eastward. We skirted the university town of Göttingen, passed prosperous, sleepy villages of half-timbered houses. As she drove, she spoke about her work with the new immigrants for ZWST.

Monika was a single mother, whose parents were German Jews. They had lived in South America for decades but had returned to Germany some years ago. She worked as a teacher and social worker in a Kassel high school, and had only recently started working for ZWST. "It gives me the chance to think about my own Jewishness," she said, "and it gives me the chance to learn along with the Russians. God knows they've got a long way to go."

The road wound its way around plump green hills, where streams gurgled in valleys and clumps of evergreen woods dotted the landscape. "This place we're going," Monika said, "is called Mackenröde, and it's terribly isolated.

"I go to school with the kids from Mackenröde sometimes, and I see what the parents mean when they say they've put all their hopes in their children. These Russian youngsters have such drive, they are so determined to succeed, you can just feel it. Oh sure, you get the occasional teenager who just wants to loaf and do nothing, but I'd say the majority are intent on getting ahead." She turned to me. "I suppose there is something to this Jewish love of education, wouldn't you agree?" (I thought back to my own university days and wasn't so sure...)

At some point we crossed the old East German border, but neither of us could spot just where. Driving a bit further on, tucked into its own lonely little valley and guarded by a row of poplars was a four-storey barracks that used to belong to the East German border police.

Inside a meeting room on the ground floor, two long tables made of shiny blonde veneer – standard East German issue – were pushed together. Polyester lace curtains hung stiff as stalactites from the windows, and twenty-eight people sat around the table. They ranged in age from five to sixty although there were no teenagers in sight. Someone had prepared a large batch of fried doughnuts sprinkled with powdered sugar. Steam curled up from them as well as from two pitchers of tea steeping nearby. Monika stood at the front before a board on which she had written words such as Yom Kippur and Fasting. She spoke in English. A thirtyish man from Kiev, Boris Press, translated for her. His English was perfect, far better than his German.

Today's discussion was about Yom Kippur and its significance. How this is the one day of the year Jews atone for their sins. That it is the holiest day of the year in the Jewish calendar. "You begin with the ancient prayer Kol Nidre, a very famous melody," said Monika.

"Now Kol Nidre is the prayer that came from the Marranos, and it is the prayer that absolves you from any false promises or pledges or allegiances you have made, or were forced to make during the year." She turned to Boris. "I'm sorry, do you know who the Marranos were?"

He nodded, then rattled off an explanation to the others in Russian. I heard the words Christopher Columbus. Everyone around the table nodded sagely.

"What did you just say?" Monika asked.

"I said what everybody knows," Boris explained. "That the Marranos were Jews who stayed in Spain after the expulsion and hid their religion and took vows of Christianity, and that Christopher Columbus was Jewish, a Marrano."

Monika looked a bit taken aback. Everyone was beaming at her as if the fact was obvious. So Monika called down to me at the far end of the table. "Do you know anything about this?"

"Sure," I said. "It's from the same book that says Shakespeare was Jewish."

Boris Press said, "Oh, and I suppose he wasn't?"

Monika Domaij-Gaul giving a lesson in Jewish customs and traditions in a barracks in Mackenröde in the former East Germany. September 1995.

Monika skipped the Jewish discovery of America and went back to Yom Kippur. She spoke of the seriousness of the day and she did so eloquently, with examples and stories. Finally she spoke of the Notana Tokesh, and talked of the prayer that says that on this day, the Book of Judgment is opened, and on this day everyone's fate is decided: who shall live and who shall die, who shall fall by fire and who by sword, who shall fall ill and who shall recover.

When she finished, the room was quiet.

Silver-haired Efim Kislenko had been in Germany six months. He came from Zhitomir, in the Ukraine. "Well, are we going to be able to come to synagogue on Yom Kippur? You just said you can't drive. Does that mean ZWST won't send a bus for us?"

"That's right, I'm afraid. They just won't, not on this day."

"Well pardon me for saying this," Efim said, "but it hardly seems fair. I mean, you're telling us all this, we're learning – really for the first time – how to be Jews, and then we hear we can't even go to a synagogue on this important day." He looked around and a few heads nodded in agreement.

"I have a question," said sixty-eight year old Ida Weintraub, from Kiev. She waited until she had everyone's attention. "How come it is that we Jews are – " she stopped, drew in her breath, then let it out – "simply hated? I ask you, Miss Monika. Are we such sinners? Have we done anything so terrible I don't know about or can't comprehend other than to just be Jewish? Why? We go to shul – they hate us. We don't go to shul – they still hate us." She slapped the table for emphasis. "You explain to me why we are hated."

For a brief moment, absolute silence. Everyone stared wide-eyed at each other. Then there was an explosion of chatter, each person unleashing a hundred and one stories, affirmations, remembrances, grievances. Just as suddenly, it all stopped and everyone turned back to Monika.

Monika Domaij-Gaul shrugged. Boris shrugged.

Sinaiola Tschushmir, from Russia, sat with her eight year old daughter on her lap. "Well, all I know is that our parents knew everything about Judaism, how to live like a Jewish family. But because of Communism, we learned nothing from them. Now that generation is gone, we've learned nothing, and now we're sitting here." She raised her voice and flashed her eyes around the table. "We know nothing!

"So what I want to know is, okay, it may be too late for me, but who will teach my daughter here how to be a good Jew, because it's not too late for her, is it?"

"Monika," she said as she clutched her child, "is there some special prayer you can say in your synagogue for me so my daughter will be Jewish?" Freeing one hand, Siniaola Tschushmir reached for a handkerchief and dabbed her eyes. She looked utterly sad. She looked lost.

It was painful and frustrating for these people to try to latch on to their religion and roots in such a place as Mackenröde. While the *Zentralrat* and ZWST tried to get the various state and federal ministries to see the light and so that they would send the Jewish immigrants to larger cities, there was little that could be done in a country of perenniel housing shortages and steep real estate prices. These Jews were being allowed into Germany and were being treated to a comprehensive social welfare system. That was generous in itself. But in barracks and ready-made shoe box-sized containers, many were sitting and hoping for the chance to move to bigger cities, where they could, for the first time in their lives, live as Jews inside a Jewish community.

Russian student learning German in a Berlin high school. June 1992.

Not all communities in the big cities laid out a welcome mat for them, but most did. Michael Szentei-Heise, executive director of the Düsseldorf Jewish community, showed me around the office where immigrants were being processed. Sitting at a table in front of a small metal box, he said, "We start here." He took the Russian passport of a Mr Snajpermann from a plastic folder, held it inside the box and flicked on an ultra-violet light. It was the same machine used by border police at airports to detect forgeries. "Sorry to say," he said, "but we've found over one hundred fake applications – Russians getting into Germany as Jews. I mean, you have to expect it, what with conditions over there. They do the same trying to get into the US, so this machine," he said as he turned off the light and patted it, "is our insurance policy." He slid Snajpermann's documents back into their folder and smiled. "A new commu-

nity member. As kosher as they come." On the floor above, several families were waiting to be interviewed by community workers. Upon arriving in Düsseldorf, new immigrants are put into temporary housing, taken to a series of seminars of instruciton, handed language schools certificates and then given the address of the Jewish community center on Zieten Strasse.

There Sonja Vengerova was their first contact. Born in Moscow, she moved to Germany six years ago. Her job was to help immigrants enroll their children into the Jewish kindergarten or elementary school and to explain to them the various community programs available. She also helped secure places for children and teenagers in the ZWST summer camp and sports activities.

In the next office sat Melita Neumann, whose job it was to help new community members integrate better into German society. Melita came from a German-speaking village in Soviet Moldova twenty years ago, was trained as a social worker and spent five years resettling ethnic Germans from the ex-Soviet Union for the Red Cross. She knew who could solve which problems, which bureaucrats would help and which she avoided. Melita spent three afternoons a week visiting the barracks and apartments where the new arrivals lived, showing them how to cope – from getting teeth filled to filling out bank forms, from arranging extra language lessons to looking for apartments.

In May 1996, Melita and Sonja arranged a meeting for me with Igor Raskin and his wife Nina Kovarskaja.

Nina's father came from a shtetl in the Ukraine and was one of the few in his family who survived the Holocaust. Determined to leave his Judaism behind, he married a non-Jewish woman and did not raise his daughter Jewish. "It didn't help," Nina

Russian Jewish couple painting their newly-acquired apartment in Magdeburg. August 1992.

said. "We were Jewish in the eyes of everyone else."

Nina, an English teacher, met Igor Raskin, an engineer in 1983. They married the following year and settled in Moscow. His parents came from shtetls in Belorus and "my name had me branded as a Jew from the outset." With the birth of their children, Stanislav in 1985 and Irina in 1988, Igor said, "both Nina and I realized we wanted our children to live Jewish. My sister was already living in Düsseldorf, so we decided to give it a try." They arrived on 27 September 1994

Igor and Nina went to the Jewish community and submitted their papers for approval. Nina was told that since her mother was not Jewish, she could not be considered Jewish. She was stunned. "I had spent my whole life being persecuted and pushed down because I was a Jew," she said, "and now I was told I'm not. So I asked if it is possible for me to convert, and if it was possible for our children to join the Jewish community. They told us yes, and for that, I'm very happy."

Nina shuffled on her chair and adjusted her pocketbook on her lap. "Irina now goes to the It-zhak Rabin elementary school, she's in first grade, and the very first day she came home from school, she ran into the apartment and shouted, 'Shalom!' Can you imagine?"

"She's growing up completely normal – as a Jewish child. She's learning Hebrew prayers, she's doing well in school, and it's she who's teaching us how to be Jewish. She's the one bringing all the Yiddishkeit home." Nina Raskin stopped for a moment, then said slowly, evenly, as if she were trying the concept out: "Our daughter is proud to be a Jew."

Not long after Stanislav was enrolled in the Evangelical school ("he's too old for the Jewish school, but they know he's Jewish and are sensitive to that," said Nina), he took sick, and doctors diagnosed diabetes. "It came as a shock, and it means we have to look at everything differently. Stanislav is so active and he uses so much energy that we worry. In his day care center, well, they couldn't be more kind. They cook for him special every day." Nina shook her head. "But it did mean that instead of Sunday school at the Jewish community, we keep him home and resting."

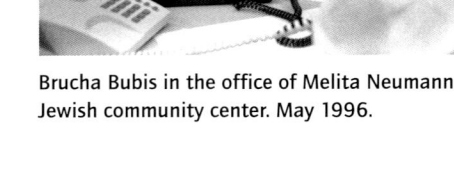

Brucha Bubis in the office of Melita Neumann in the Düsseldorf Jewish community center. May 1996.

Nina and Igor have been looking for work. "But it's so very hard. My diploma as a translator and teacher are useless. Whatever you do here, you must have a paper proving you're qualified. And that takes years to get. To accept welfare, well, it's humiliating. But Igor and I have to face it, our professional lives have come to an end.

"We have talked everything over, and we've decided I have a bit better chance than he does. I've applied to go to an advanced level language school, and I'll travel to Dortmund by train while Igor stays home for the children. I've only recently come to understand how much the odds are against my working, but I just won't accept it. I'm going to learn this language, and I'm going to get a job."

Nina looked at her watch, then said something to Igor. "Excuse us, but Irina will be coming home from school soon. I have to tell you one more thing. Yesterday she stood with me in the kitchen and gave me a whole list of things we have to do without now – food, I mean." A proud mother's face brightened. "Our daughter, she's making us Jewish."

Of the twenty-something thousand Russians who have arrived in Germany the past few years, how many want to be Jewish like the Raskins? To raise their children with a Jewish consciousness? Most estimates suggest that somewhere between fifteen and twenty percent wish to reconnect to their religion, not more.

"But look here in Dortmund," Hans Frankenthal, an Auschwitz survivor told me one night after Friday night services in June 1996. The hall was filled with fifty teenagers. "We've now got two thousand Russians living around this area. If we get ten percent, ten percent thank you, then we'll have two hundred Jews at Friday night services. And we can barely fit that many in! "

Robbie, fifteen years old, red-haired, and athletic looking, said, "We get fifty kids in our youth center now – fifty!" When I asked how many they would get without the Russians, he threw his head back and laughed "Maximum?" he asked back.

"Maximum," I replied.

"Five, including me."

The task of turning children into Jews belongs to the communities as well as ZWST. And ZWST entrusted the task to Deni Kranz. Deni was born in Cologne to Israeli parents in 1965. In that year they returned to Israel but came back when he was five. Settling in Frankfurt, his father worked for the Jewish Agency and his mother taught in Frankfurt's Jewish school. Deni grew up completely within the

Actress from St. Petersburg in her hotel room in Frankfurt/Main. June 1992.

Jewish community and by the time he was sixteen years, he was acting as a counselor, one of the madrachim, of ZWST.

Combining his interest in Jewsih life with his interest in pedagogical studies, Deni worked in ZWST youth programs as he earned his bachelors and masters degrees. In 1994 he started on a doctorate and was hired by ZWST to work full time. "I decided to write my thesis on the absorption of Ethiopian Jews in Israel because I find it fascinating how outsiders who don't fit into a society are integrated. But in 1995 I changed it to the absorption of Russian Jews in Germany. I mean, the way I figure it," he added sadly, "we have our own Ethiopians right here – outsiders, unwelcomed. You can believe me, not all the communities are so helpful. I send out offers to bring the kids to a seminar, but when I follow up, the communities tell me none of their Russian Jews is interested. You know what I say? Bullshit."

Tirza Hodes teaching Israeli folk dancing to new immigrants. Berlin, November 1995.

Spending time in the community centers, attending seminars and lectures, going to Sobernheim and synagogue and taking trips to Israel together have, according to Deni Kranz, created new Jews. "You have to see it to believe it," he said, inviting me to attend a weekend get-together for Jewish youth in Berlin in November 1995. He was expecting sixty people, and more than half of them would be recent immigrants.

It was a typical November night in Berlin. It hadn't rained, but the cobblestones of the old Jewish quarter sweated moisture, the bare trees glistened, and the stubborn fog that had sat on the city all day long hadn't budged. In the Jewish community center on Oranienburger Strasse, Deni was conducting a Friday night service to a packed room of teenagers. He and two teenagers led the service, and when it was finished, everyone filed down the hall and into the private dining room of the ad-

joining kosher-style restaurant, *Café Oren*, where an Israeli-style buffet dinner had been laid out for them: humus and falafel, eggplant salads and taboule and pita bread. Seventeen year old Viktor, from a small town near Kiev, stood with a plate in his hand, a fork poised over the buffet, and had no idea what to do. "My God," gasped eighteen year old Jana, from Riga, standing beside him, eyeing the strange-looking food. Both of them had been in Germany less than six months. The other new arrivals were equally mystified, but hunger led to experimentation.

When the last falafel had been tucked into its pita and eaten, as the dishes were being taken away, Deni introduced the group to two Israelis who would be working with them that weekend. One was Moshe, a jovial, silver-haired character. He would lead them in Israeli songs and accompany them on his accordion. Tirza, a beaming seventy year old, who originally came from Düsseldorf, would teach Israeli folk dancing.

After his eyes scanned the room, Deni Kranz smiled and said, "You know, once upon a time – and I don't know if you'll remember, there-was-this-great-big-wall." He enunciated the words very slowly. Giggles all around. He smiled, then added. "But no more. And right after that, I started seeing some new faces at our programs. And tonight, I see some of the same faces I saw over five years ago. And I'm smiling because right now, I also see some faces I haven't known for more than five minutes. So let's begin this weekend by speaking about those of us who have been here the longest, because sometimes, we need to be reminded." Deni raised his voice ever-so slightly, and the points he was making found their mark on the faces of those around the table. "Reminded of how few friends we had when we first came to Berlin. Reminded of how little we knew of Judaism, of Yiddishkeit." His voice suddenly softened. "But we worked together.

Surrounded by newly-arrived teenagers from the ex-Soviet Union, Deni Kranz conducts a Havdalah service, commemorating the end of the Jewish Sabbath. Berlin, November 1995.

Moshe here came from Israel and taught us songs. Tirza came and we learned how to dance. Others taught us Hebrew and still others taught us religion and tradition and – and, guess what? Now we really, really know how to be Jewish. And I have to say: that's not so bad.

"But now, I see we are joined by more and more new immigrants. And here we are, just arrived in this big, rich, confusing land where we are outsiders, foreigners, and," he raised his hand and counted off on his fingers, "we don't have apartments, and we don't have cars, and we don't have good German yet, and we are right back in the same place that we were five years ago. "Now I'm not saying that everyone who's been here a few years has to walk every new immigrant through every trial and every tribulation, no. I'm saying that for those of us who know more, it should feel good to help someone new. It should feel good to be," he paused, then created a word of his own, combining Hebrew, Yiddish and German – "menschlichim – and therefore, what I encourage us all to do, whether you have been here one year, two years, or five years, please: Let's all help each other. After all, every one of us is Jewish, and that means every one of us knows what it means to be a refugee. Because my friends, that's how it's been for Jews for a long, long time."

From then until Sunday evening, over bagels and lox, coffee and cake, babaganoush and another mountain of falafel, thirty newly-arrived teenagers danced with Tirza, sang with Moshe, listened to, argued with and discussed matters with Deni. On Saturday morning, twenty of them traipsed behind Yossi Vardi, the ZWST Berlin director, to synagogue. "This Viktor, he stood next to me so close he was almost on top of me," Yossi said smiling. "His mouth was so wide open I could have lost my car in it. And you know, afterwards as we walked back here, he asked me so many questions and kept asking, 'so when can I come back, when can I get to join a real community like this?'"

During a lull in the programming, I sat with three girls. Gena came from Dnjepropetrowsk. At seventeen, she had been in Germany for five years. Her father was already working as a shoemaker and her mother had an office job. She was sitting next to Veronika, eighteen years old, from Lvov. Both of Veronika's parents were also working – her father was a building supervisor, her mother an architect. Julia, eighteen, had been in Berlin since 1991. She came from Moscow and was about to graduate high school. Her parents also had jobs. "My mother's a music teacher and my father's a basketball referee, and I want to study economics."

Newly-arrived family from Moscow in a barracks in Eisleben. July 1992.

Hanukkah dance at the Jewish Cultural Society, Berlin. December 1994.

Hanukkah dance at the Jewish Cultural Society, Berlin. December 1994.

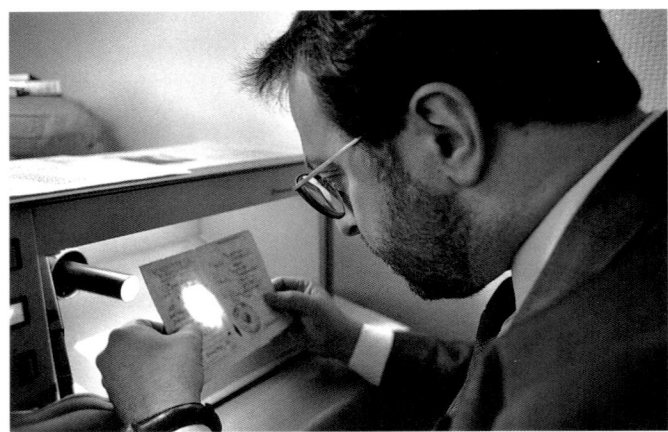

Michael Szentei-Heise, director of the Düsseldorf Jewish community center, scrutinizing, under ultra-violet light, the papers of a newly-arrived Russian Jew. More than 100 forgeries were discovered on this machine. May 1996.

Newly arrived Soviet immigrant waiting before an administration window in Munich. August 1992.

Junj Marchowsky, from Kiev, arriving in Cologne with his grandsons, Ilia and Michael. June 1992.

We lost our home.
We lost our childhood

If you travel to western Palatinate in Germany's Rhineland, to the steep river valleys where the temperatures are mild and vineyards string the hills with green lace, you will find three prim wine villages nestled together along the Mosel: Alf, Bullay and Zell. Here white-washed houses crowned with black slate roofs cluster on cobbled squares. Wine cellars serve hearty regional fare and the loudest sounds on autumn afternoons are those of bottles uncorking and glasses clinking. Erna Dorn (born Kaufmann) and her cousin Gerda Gardner (also born Kaufmann) came from one of those villages: Alf. Walter Kahn and his brother Ernst grew up just across the river in Bullay, and downstream, in Zell, Fritz Bender and his sister Marta were born. Lee Kahn's family (the Adlers) also came from Zell but moved to Cologne just before Lee was born. I met these seven people in September 1995. What made them different from other *Moselaners* was that sixty years ago, they were hounded out of their schools and jobs and chased out of the country. They left behind family members who were shipped away by neighbors and killed in Germany's name. After the war, none of these seven came home to live. They settled in Canada, Israel and the United States. Now these former citizens of Alf, Bullay and Zell were returning as officially invited guests.

During their week along the Mosel, most of the group stayed in Haus Waldfrieden, a whimsical old pension built on a vine-covered hill overlooking a bend in the river. It was owned by Dr. Ullrich Stein, a fortyish biologist turned vintner. Ulli, as his

Walter Kahn with Marie. September 1995.

guests affectionately called him, woke early each morning, and after laying out breakfast, donned his knee-high rubber boots, and waded out into his beloved vineyards. Walter Kahn, eighty-five years old, sipped his coffee and watched him from the terrace.

Walter and I would meet over breakfast, and as the sun burnt off the morning fog, as black and white barges made their way along the Mosel toward Koblenz, Walter would reminisce. His brother Ernst often joined us, and together, they pieced together their family history, a history that had begun along the Mosel when Napoleon ruled it and ended one hundred-thirty years later just before Hitler invaded France.

The only thing Ernst and Walter knew of their great-great-grandfather Josef Sondheimer was that he arrived in the valley during the early 1800s. He settled in Zell, married Ris Reis and was the first Jew in modern times to be buried in the Jewish cemetery of Bullay, a few kilometers downriver. His grave, worn and barely legible now, reads 1831 and nearly butts up against the picket fence, as if it is trying to peer down to the river below.

When Josef and Ris lived in Zell, there was no synagogue and no organized Jewish community in any of the three villages. But their son Moses (born 1811), who grew up to sell grapes to vintners and traded sometimes in cattle and leather, saw the building of a tiny synagogue in Zell in 1848. By then, some fifty Jews had settled in the valley.

Moses's son Adam was born in the eventful year of 1848. To the west, riots swept another Napoleon to power. There were riots calling for democratic reform in the German states and duchies as well, but they were soon swept aside by the powers of re-action and conservatism. As Adam grew toward adulthood, a customs union forged closer links between the German states, and when he was seventeen years old in 1866, he watched with awe as Prussia's chancellor Bismarck fought the Austrian Kaiser to establish Berlin's hegemony over Vienna. Four years later, Adam Sondheimer donned a uniform himself and went to war against France. By the time he returned home – as a sergeant – the German states were united into a single empire, ruled by Prussia's Hohenzollerns and Bismarck himself. Every year after that, a proud and fiercely patriotic Adam Sondheimer, in his neatly-pressed uniform, marched in the annual veterans parade through Zell and Bullay. When he opened a clothing store in 1873, he placed an ad in the local newspaper stating that "the war veteran Adam Sondheimer welcomes all old and new friends to his haberdashery." He married Babett Thormann a few years later. Their daughter Emma was born in 1884. Because the Jewish communities along the Mosel were so small, parties and holiday celebrations were held in central meeting points so young Jews could meet, court and hopefully marry other Jews. In 1905 Julius and Babette sent Emma down river to Bad Betrich for a Purim ball. There she danced with Julius Kahn, who came from a family of cattle dealers in Empken, just over the hill. They fell in love, married soon after, and Julius came to Zell to live with the Sondheimers.

"He was a creative man, my father," Walter said as he watched Ulli clipping away at the vines on the hillside. "He managed to scrape up enough money to build a new house for us in Bullay. He had trained to be a butcher so he built a shop that fronted the street and we lived upstairs. In the courtyard in back, he put up a slaughterhouse and small baloney factory – kettles, pressure cookers, all that. He and my mother settled down to have children – Hans was born in 1907, I was born in 1910 and Ernst was born three years later."

When Ernst was barely one year old, word came to Bullay that the Austrian archduke was shot dead in Sarajevo. Seven weeks later Europe was at war. Adam Sondheimer, who was sixty-six years old then, must have been proud to see that his son-in-law was one of the very first to sign up for the Kaiser's army. In one of the first offensives on the eastern front, Julius took a bullet in his shoulder. He was awarded an iron cross, second class, and after a few weeks in a field hospital in Riga he was shipped home to recuperate. Ever anxious to return to the front, Julius was sent to France to fight in 1915. He was wounded slightly twice more and was awarded an iron cross first class in 1917. But in September 1918, Emma Kahn received word her husband had been badly wounded and lay in a field hospital in Strasbourg. She left the children with her parents and took the first west-bound train to be with her husband. Doctors provided a furlough and Emma brought Julius home. She began nursing him back to health while his three sons and anxoius father-in-law looked on. But as autumn set in, and the first chill winds blew down the Mosel that October, Julius Kahn's lungs congested, pneumonia set in and he died. Adam Sondheimer followed his casket up the hill, past the respectful neighbors who turned out to watch the procession. He buried his son-in-law not far from his own grandfather's grave.

The war ended a few weeks later, the Kaiser abdicated, and on November 9, Germany was declared a democracy. But no one took down the pictures of the Kaiser or Bismarck that Julius had put up just before he went off to war.

Adam Sondheimer sold his store in Zell and began making the daily trek to Bullay to work in Emma's butcher shop. He bought a horse and wagon and headed up into the Hunsrück each week, going from farm to farm, buying and trading with farmers and bringing down calves and cows.

Adam Sondheimer worried about his family. Germany was hardly the same during those Weimar days of political instability and wild inflation. He felt relieved when General Hindenburg became president of the republic in 1925. To some, perhaps, Hindenburg was an aging relic with an undeserved military reputation, but he represented stability to many Germans, and Adam Sondheimer hung the general's picture in his daughter's home, next to the other portraits. Adam Sondheimer died a few months later at the age of seventy-seven.

Ernst said, "My mother was left running everything herself. You can just imagine what that was like with three boys, but we all pitched in, although

View of the Mosel River valley from Haus Waldfrieden. September 1995.

she shipped Walter off to high school in Empken, where he stayed with our grandmother. My mother hired local people to work for us, and a cousin came too. We had five or six people working in the shop.

"Back then, when I was in elementary school, we had a great time. No difference between Jews and non-Jews – not in such a small town like this. No one here really had money; people had debts and in Bullay, which was a railroad junction, half the town worked for the railroad or the post office. Walter even remembers when they brought electricity to town, just around the First World War."

Walter smiled. Ernst went on. "Whenever there was a new birth in town, my mother would cook the family a big pot of soup and send us over with it. On weekends, we'd go for long hikes and end up right here at Haus Waldfrieden, where we would dance to music we played on a wind-up phonograph. So we could better learn our Jewish studies, we had *Der Lehrer*, as we all called him, Mr Kornfeld from Budapest. He was even poorer than the rest of us, so he would travel up and down the Mosel, going from one Jewish family to another, staying with each family for a week, teaching the children Hebrew, helping with their bar mitzvah lessons, and then he'd move on to the next family.

"Our neighbors, the Stadtfelds, were always running in and out of our house, and I was doing the same over at theirs. Matter of fact, while the three sisters there, Erna, Hilde and Eleanor, were good students, Herman, their brother, was much more into sports and working." Ernst leaned over, winked and whispered, "Don't tell the Stadtfelds, but I used to do Herman's homework for him. He never was too good with his studies." Although Ernst was the only Jewish student in school, he said he never noticed the difference. "Look," he said with a sigh. "Nearly all of us got along. Maybe this was unique, maybe not. I only knew that in our town – with a thousand residents and twenty Jews, it wasn't so hard to be nice to your neighbor." All that changed when Ernst finished school and went to work in nearby Wittlich, population 7,000.

Here was a city of some two hundred and seventy Jews and a fine, stone synagogue. This was not a hut clinging to the rich family's Schloss like in Zell, but an elegant neo-Romanesque structure where the Jews of Wittlich came wearing top hats and tails on the High Holy Days. Wittlich's main square had several businesses owned by Jews, and both Walter and Ernst worked in Wittlich. They joined Jewish clubs and went to Jewish dances. Walter, who had spent three years in Berlin, had moved to Wittlich a few months before Ernst. He showed his younger brother around, told him of the excitement going on in the awesome German capital and regaled him with Berlin tales – of boating with beautiful girls on the Wannsee, the cabarets and coffee houses and new music. But Walter knew something else. On the streets the Nazis fought Communists in pitched battles and free-for-alls. Brown-shirted thugs roamed the streets. "Not long before I left Berlin, I went to a screening of 'All Quiet on the Western Front.' The film was banned by the government, but the SPD showed it at a private screening. Naturally, it was packed, and on stage, just before the film began, Clara Zetkin, a very important socialist leader then, spoke. What a firebrand she was, and she talked about how a Germany under the Nazis would wreak a war of revenge that would bring all of Europe down. She spoke so sure and confidently that I was really shaken up. I felt the handwriting on the wall that night. And that was in 1931."

On the streets of Wittlich, the number of Nazi thugs grew, and once the federal government passed into the hands of their party, they roamed the streets singing anti-Semitic songs and breaking Jewish store windows. Wittlich Jews spoke among themselves about abandoning the country and the Kahn boys returned home to the relative quiet of Bullay. Hans, the oldest brother, and Walter, left for America in 1935 but Ernst stayed behind with his mother. "We had to stay. Over in Empken, we had my father's mother to look after, and my own mother wasn't going to leave until we had to."

After the National Socialists took power, the laws restricting the rights of Jews tightened, and customers dwindled away. "We had to let all our butchers go, so the baloney factory had to close. Later we couldn't employ any workers at all, so the shop couldn't really make it." To make ends meet, Ernst started buying up clothing and loading it into his car, taking off each evening to make sales calls on farmers along the Hunsrück.

"Everyone was friendly, I never had problems. And some friends never deserted us – like Paul Kretz. The two of us were always together, you see, going to football matches, playing sports – the best of friends. He never, not ever, stopped coming to our house, and he did it openly because he hated the Nazis. He deserted from the army in 1945 and lived out in the woods. I was already in America, and I sent him food packages those first few years after the war." Ernst smiled and shook his head. "Knowing Paul, I wasn't a bit surprised he did this." He bit his lip. "He died, though, in 1958, and I never saw him again.

In 1937 they took all our official papers away, and we couldn't work – period. So I loaded up the baloney equipment into cars and trucks – the kettles, the compressors, all that – and headed out late every evening. Somehow, I managed to sell everything off. I'm sure the chief policeman of Bullay knew all this – Mr Höfer, but he never said anything. After all, when he moved to Bullay back in the twenties, he was here for more than a year before his family joined him, and my mother fed him every night."

While friends were now shying away from Bullay's twenty Jews, a young girl named Marie came every night to help out around the Kahn home. "She was an illegitimate child and everyone in town looked down on her except my mother."

Walter said. "She was always nice to Marie, so when so many others turned away from us, Marie would come to us to help clean the house. We didn't even ask her to, but she wanted to help." The Kahns never forgot Marie's kindness.

Jewish businesses were confiscated one by one and even in these villages, old friends turned into Nazis. "Not everyone took it so quietly," Ernst said. "There was a Nazi party meeting one night and two Jewish boys, Alfred Adler and Max Wolf, ran in, smashed up everything and everyone in it, then ran out. It must have been something! But I guess they did it spontaneously because Alfred fled almost immediately for Holland although poor Max stayed behind. He realized, I guess, how tough he had made things on himself. he was frightened, morose, and one night, he slipped into his father's butcher shop in Zell, loaded the rifle his father shot cattle with, and turned it on himself."

One night around 10:00 PM, Ernst and his mother were summoned to the house of Mr Beck, head of the railroad yard in Bullay and the local Nazi big shot. "He lived in a huge house up the hill, and when we arrived, there was coffee and cake for us. This was surprising enough, but Beck said, 'Frau Kahn, it is well known you have been good and kind to everyone here, but the party wants non-Jewish butchers in Bullay and both butcher shops are owned by Jews. I want you to sell your shop to Herr Uwer – Peter Uwer – because this is how things will have to be.'

Well, my mother was just furious and she wasn't about to give up all that she'd worked for. She said she wouldn't even entertain the notion. But Mr Beck said he had even gotten permission to transfer, directly from the Nazi party, 50,000 reichsmarks – not a small sum, I can tell you. But this only made her angrier.

So he looked at me and shook his head. He showed us a whole batch of papers from the party, how they planned to take all the businesses from all the Jews, and he said, 'Ernst, I want you to talk to your mother. She can sell me the business, or I can take it. But either way, I'm going to get it.' And even though my mother was a very good business woman, she refused to take money from the Nazi party. If they were going to take our property, they weren't going to do it with my mother's help. 'This has nothing to do with money,' she said as we walked down the hill. She stuck to her word, too."

Within months, Mr Beck had installed Mr Uwer and the last of the Kahns prepared to leave the Mosel valley. Walter and Hans had American visas

Walter Kahn and other former Jewish residents of Alf, Bullay and Zell visiting the former Zell synagogue. September 1995.

arranged for them. Ernst and his mother went to see Julius Kahn's mother, who would not discuss leaving her home. Ernst went to the bank in Empken and arranged to have his father's military pension sent to her account every month. "That's what kept her alive," he said, his voice cracking, "all the way until they came and shipped her to Auschwitz at ninety-four years old." His mother sold the house – "for a pittance, I can tell you" – to the Stadtfelds. Just before the Kahns caught the afternoon train out of Bullay, they climbed through the vineyards above the Mosel and swung open the gate to the Jewish cemetery. They stood before Josef's grave, then paid their respects before the stones for Moses, Adam and Julius. They turned and left. The date was August 1937. Ernst Kahn was twenty-four years old. Fifteen months later the synagogues in Wittlich and Zell were ransacked, and those Jews who had not left were desperate enough to try anything to get out. Of the twenty Bullay Jews in 1930, seven were deported, the rest made it to safety. Across the river, ten of Alf's eleven Jews escaped, leaving one behind for neighbors to deport. Of Zell's thirty-two Jews, eighteen left in time. Of those who could not

Gerda Gardner, née Kaufmann, in the Wittlich Jewish Museum, where she sees photographs of her childhood friends. September 1995.

Erna Dorn, née Kaufmann, points to names of friends who died in the Holocaust. September 1995.

escape, three chose suicide. No Jew returned to live in Bullay, Zell, Alf or Wittlich after the war.

An eighty-three year old Ernst Kahn stood looking over at the cemetery. He pointed to the town half submerged in trees below. "See that house there, just through the trees? That belonged to the Harfs. Arthur Harf left with my brother Hans. Julius left soon after. They moved to Erie, Pennsylvania. Now their father, Gustav, remarried after their mother died back when the boys were still young. He had the other butcher shop in Bullay and everyone in town loved old man Harf. Of course they deported him and his second wife. Killed." Turning to Walter, Ernst said, "By the way, you know who took the Harfs to the train?"

Walter nodded. "Sure I know. Mr Höfer, the policeman."

"Now if you look down a bit," Ernst went on, "that's where the Salamons, the cattle dealers, Julius and Emma, lived. Their son Oskar moved to Hamburg and he was deported, too. He survived, emigrated to Chicago and went into the carpet cleaning business. Alfred and his parents got out in 1938. Moved to Argentina."

By this time, everyone had filtered downstairs. Breakfast had been served, eaten, taken away. The fog had lifted, insects buzzed, and the snipping of Ulli's shears went on without a pause. Angelika Schleindel walked briskly into the house to fetch Walter, Ernst, Ernst's wife Thea and the rest of the crew, still lingering over coffee.

Angelika, who lived upstairs in a rambling rooftop atelier in Haus Waldfrieden, was a historian who had almost single-handedly detailed the history of the Jews of Wittlich in a book and exhibition and was now doing the same for the Mosel villages. This official visit was taking place at her instigation, and she had been in contact with Walter and Ernst for years, digging through their vast memories and archives. Angelika was acting as combination hostess, chauffeur and mother to the group, and she immediately began directing them into waiting cars. They had to hurry to Zell.

In one car, Walter was chatting with Gerda, a widow who lived in New York and had never been back to Germany until this week. She was having a bumpy time remembering things. "Hey Walter," she said, poking his arm, "what's this I hear about us going walking on the Hindenburg? I don't remember walking on any Hindenburg."

Walter laughed and said, "No Gerda, not Hindenburg – the Marienburg, where the old castle was."

Gerda shrugged. "So who can remember? Hindenburg, Marienburg, this place is full of burgs." Turning to me, Gerda said, "You have a car?"

I nodded.

"Good," she said, and gave me a couple of pokes in the shoulder. "Then you will take me into Alf. I want to go find my house. Erna!" she called.

Erna, who was talking to Angelika, turned. "Yes?"

"You'll come with me to Alf?"

"Sure, Gerda, I'd be glad to. It's what cousins are for."

I asked Gerda how it felt for her to be here. She started to say something, opened her mouth and closed it. Gathering her thoughts, she said, "Oh, I don't know, it's confusing. I haven't spoken a word of German for years, I have my worries about Germans, but now, everyone's so nice to me. Would I come back? No, I don't think so. I mean, who needs all this? Even though everyone in my family made it out of here in 1939, I still don't know. And anyway," she said as we pulled into a parking lot in Zell and she stared at two matronly women standing nearby. "Are the Germans the same? Or have they ge-changed? I mean changed? I mean, my English and German are getting all mixed up!"

Gerda didn't wait for my answer, but hoisted herself out of the car and headed through the alleyways of Zell, past the ice cream stands, the wine cellars, the souvenir shops, the tourists poking about. The Jewish group had already assembled on the back alley behind the Schloss and together with the mayor, a few local dignitaries and a camera crew, they entered the tiny synagogue. This single visible monument to Zell's Jewish past was in poor condition, a dusty little room closed up and used as a storehouse.

Slowly entering the room on his cane, Walter said without looking around, "You'll notice there's a plaque for Zell Jews killed in the First World War, but that's where history stops." He frowned and searched around for a chair to sit on. "I wrote a letter to the mayor and asked that they turn this place into a museum, a memorial, but he wrote back and said the city council voted it down." He shook his head. "I'm not surprised, but I think in time, the next generation will have the courage to right this wrong. The old ones just don't want to be reminded, that's all."

In the tiny synagogue, the seven Jews and their families reminisced. Fritz Bender and his sister Marta, together with their own children, spoke quietly among themselves. Lee and her two sons read the names off the plaque. Gerda pointed up to the tiny balcony. "Hey, that's where we used to have sat, the girls and our mothers. But just look at this place! It looks terrible!"

As her eyes swept the crowd, she said, "You know, the people around here, they broke everything in the synagogue on *Kristallnacht*. We were still living in Alf, just across the river. Well, we never came back here after that. We were afraid."

The television camera crept around like a giant plastic bird, dipping its snout into the old Jews' faces. The TV light burned brightly as two school children unveiled a wooden plaque with the names of those killed during the Holocaust. At this, Walter smiled.

Later that day there was a meeting at the town

hall. Speeches were made by politicians and clergymen. Some seemed cut out of wood. Others were powerful, emotionally driven. Afterwards, bottles of locally grown wine were given out along with coffee table books about Zell. Ernst's wife Thea (born Ladenburger in a small town in the Black Forest) smiled. "I'll tell you the truth. It's easy to be a Jew in Germany for a week. Longer than that, well, it's not for me."

During the week of their visit, the Alf, Zell and Bullay Jews went to see their old homes, looked up records and spoke with school children. I accompanied them to one high school down river in Cochem, but we stopped, as promised, in Alf, so Gerda could look around. Not quite as picture-perfect as Zell, it was every bit as tidy. Gerda made her way straight down a narrow lane toward her old house, steaming ahead of Erna and me. Just before reaching the house, an elderly couple stepped out into the street and nearly bumped into her. The man spotted Gerda and turned to his wife and said, "Ah, here's Gerda Kaufmann. How are you Gerda?" And he said it as if she had simply been out of town for the weekend. This made Gerda cackle and the three of them smiled. "Well, I'm just fine. But who are you?" She squinted at them as if narrowing her vision would melt the wrinkles from their faces, the years from her memory.

While the three old neighbors caught up, Erna said, "Our family came from Alf, too. But my father bought a small store in Bad Bertrich when I was young, so we moved. It's not far from here, just a nice summer resort town with baths and springs. It wasn't very fancy, not on the lines of the great spas then like Marienbad or Karlsbad. It was more middle class – nice, sure – but most patients came on their insurance bills. My father died in 1919 during the influenza epidemic, so my mother and two brothers had to run our small dry goods store. We were the only Jewish family in town and we learned our Hebrew and everything Jewish from *Der Lehrer*, poor Mr Kornfeld. I think he taught Gerda, too."

By then Gerda's old neighbors had moved on and she turned to face her old home. It had been prettified and replastered and double-pane swing-out windows had been installed. Window boxes crowded with geraniums guarded each window.

"My my," Gerda said leaning back to take it all in. "They've certainly done a better job than we did with it!" She turned to us. "You know, if my older brother hadn't secretly sent all our money out of the country before *Kristallnacht*, my mother would have refused to leave. I mean that and she even said so." She turned back to the house and shook her head. "And if she wouldn't have gone, I wouldn't have gone and I wouldn't be here now for my nice visit." She looked at us and raised her eyebrows. The sound of a motor scooter on another alleyway echoed through the village.

The village of Cochem is even prettier than Zell and is so overwhelmed with tourists that cars aren't allowed in the summer months to climb the zig-zag alleys that wind between the half-timbered houses. The high school is wedged in a leafy ravine above the town and while Erna and Gerda went to speak to one class, Lee Adler and her two sons went off to another. Walter and Ernst would speak to the entire school a little later.

Gerda kept mumbling as she walked the halls, "What am I supposed to say to these kids? What can I say? Here we are, the Jews? The Jews are here?" Erna said nothing. She looked nervous. Angelika delivered them into a classroom of seventeen year olds.

I counted twenty students, half boys, half girls. The one boy with a pony tail wore Doc Martens. All the rest had shorter hair and sported Reeboks and Nikes. All twenty wore jeans and sweat shirts, some with hoods.

Gerda and Erna began haltingly, and told of their lives, that they were born in Alf, that they had felt part of the society for years, and suddenly, they were cast out by their friends – just, as a matter of fact, when they were the ages of the young people in this room.

"Well, how did that make you feel? I mean, did you feel German or Jewish?" one girl asked, emphasizing the or.

Erna looked surprised. "We – we were German. German, of course. Our family had been here for hundreds and hundreds of years. Jewish was our religion, that's all, but we were very, very German."

"And you were integrated into everyday society, just like everyone else, no different?" the same girl asked again.

Gerda and Erna taking a walk among the vineyards above the Mosel.

"No different than anyone. We were not religious Jews. We didn't wear black like the Hasidic
Jews do or maybe like you've seen in Fiddler on the
Roof. Most Jews in Germany were completely integrated like that. We didn't dress or look different
than anyone else."

"Then how –?" the girl asked again, but out of
frustration, she couldn't finish the sentence,
couldn't figure the whole thing out, and she raised
her hands, dropped them, then blew away a strand
of hair from her face.

Erna went on. "Suddenly, we couldn't go to the
movies." She paused, and sat for a second as if she
were allowing all the injustices to pile up inside
her. "We could not go to school, the theater, the

parks. We couldn't have a radio. Had to shop at certain times. Couldn't use public transport. One rule
after the other. And I was the only Jewish girl in
our town, so believe me, I was about –" she sighed.
"I was about as lonely as you could get."

"But in America, there are also Nazis!" said one
boy.

The teacher frowned. Erna smiled indulgently.
Gerda squinted. "I don't think I'd want to compare,"
she said flatly. "Get your history straight." Yet she
said it without rancor.

The questions came rapidly. "How does it feel to
return?" "Difficult, but in some ways, it still feels
like home." "Do you have any German friends?" "In
America, many of our friends are other German

Jews." "Do you hate Germany?" "Hate?" repeated Erna. She considered for a moment. "No, I don't hate Germany. But my mother was killed by Germans."

At the end of their talk, Erna and Gerda went down the stairs surrounded by girls from the class. At the bottom of the steps they halted and kept on talking for another five minutes. When they scampered off, Erna came up to me beaming. "Oh they are really such nice girls! So poised and intelligent. Now I'm reminded of going to school and how much I loved it," then, lowering her voice, "before they threw me out, of course. And friends! They have so many friends." Erna watched them congregating and chatting away in the courtyard. "I was so alone when I was their age, so alone." Gerda, who had been listening to Erna as she watched the kids outside, said, almost absently, "We lost our home. We lost our childhood."

All the students gathered in a large room where Walter and Ernst were sitting. Erna and Gerda, Lee and her sons, joined them. Reinhold Schommers, principal of the school and the prime mover in bringing the elderly Jews to his students, stood between the two and spoke with passion and energy of the importance of this visit and the unique chance it was for the students of Cochem to talk with those who had lived through so much – so much history, so much tragedy.

If the words sounded boilerplate, they were not. Schommers was deadly serious about engaging his students in historical and political dialogue. Indeed, the Cochem high school was a hotbed of humanitarian aid for Bosnia, and these students raised funds, gathered clothes and food and shipped it to refugee camps throughout ex-Yugoslavia.

The elderly Jews addressed the fresh-faced youths. Ernst Kahn was particularly gentle when he spoke of the past. He said he didn't blame his friends and neighbors for what happened as they had no choice but to avoid their Jewish friends. The pressure was too great during the Third Reich and Ernst clearly differentiated between his neighbors and Nazis. "People had to go along or lose their jobs," he explained. Erna spoke of how lonely she felt, how her friends turned on her. Lee spoke of her aunt Elsa, who cared for her every day while her parents went out to try and scrape together enough income to feed the family, and how Elsa was deported to Minsk and starved to death there.

What the elderly Jews tried to get across was that this scenic river valley had been as much a part of their lives as it was for these kids now. Again and again, posed in different ways, the students asked, Do you hate Germans? Is it hard for you to be here? Can you forgive Germany? Is America better for you now than Germany was before the Nazis? And to Walter, one student asked, "But what was it like for you, a German, to be in America during the Second World War, when the Americans were fighting the Germans?"

"We weren't Americans, that's for sure," he replied. "But we were no longer Germans either, and most people understood that. You see, it was hard for Americans back then, for everyone – after all, this was still the Depression and so many people were out of work and had very little to share. But I have to say that from the time we arrived, America was ready to help us start over. It's kind of a philosophy there. They don't care what you've lost, what you've left behind even if we did, or maybe what I left behind –" and he suddenly started crying. Covering his eyes with hand, he said, "what I left behind, here –" The room was still. Outside, birds chirped, trees rustled in the breeze.

There were other visits: to schools, old homes, to fancy restaurants. The old Mosel Jews pulled out whole chapters of their lives and shared them with whoever was sitting next to them. Fritz Bender told me of studying in the university of Darmstadt, how when he would come home during breaks Emma Kahn would feed him in her kitchen in Bullay before he caught the narrow-gauge local train for Zell. Fritz also spoke proudly of his life as a scientist in Canada and how he helped with the war effort in the 1940s. He told me of his escape by boat from Holland in 1940 and rescue at sea by the British and how he was interned for a while as a prisoner of war. But later, Angelika told me a sadder story. Fritz had emigrated in 1933 to Holland with his wife, child and mother-in-law. When the Germans invaded in 1940, they were separated. Fritz ended up on a boat, but his wife, hearing that he was dead, and having watched the Nazis taking Jews away, killed her mother, her child and herself.

Cochem high school students listening to the former Jewish residents of the Mosel valley. September 1995.

While watching the lights of Bullay wink at us one night as we sat in an oak-paneled restaurant, Erna told me how her mother had helped her children get out of Germany, but how when she herself went to get an American visa in Stuttgart, her eyesight was so bad she was turned down. So she left Bad Bertrich and rented a room with her sister in Trier, where they waited, frightened, for the knock on the door that would take them to their deaths. It was clear that Erna had never forgiven herself for leaving her mother behind, and at eighty-years old, the memory, and the wound, was still fresh. Erna had married a Jewish refugee from Vienna, "a wonderful dancer" and had one son. They had lived in

New York, but after her husband died, Erna moved to Ft. Lauderdale. She didn't speak of her son that evening. All she could think of was her mother.

Two years previously, during an official visit to the town of Wittlich, instigated by its mayor, Helmut Hagedorn, Walter Kahn met a precocious twelve-year old called Hannes Schmit. The two became fast friends (neither Walter, whose wife died a few years ago, nor Ernst ever had children). Walter and Hannes met up again when the group visited Wittlich's synagogue (now a Jewish museum Angelika helped curate). At a dinner in a folksy Wittlich restaurant, Hannes wedged a chair between Walter and some other adults, and sat

Lee Kahn, née Adler, addressing Cochem high school students. September 1995.

there, all blue eyes and blond hair, beaming as he drank in the old man and his stories, his hand movements, his passion. Someone asked Walter, "How do you feel?" and Walter replied, "Like eighty-five years old," and Hannes nearly fell off his chair laughing. Walter reached over and rubbed the boy's head. "I just love him," Hannes said to me in a nearly-perfect American accent.

"Sure, maybe he's really old but he doesn't ever complain about his health or that kinda stuff. He's always so nice and cheerful and he's taken me all over Wittlich and showed me his town – Jewish Witlich. That's what's important, you know, to learn about the past and for him to talk to the young

people like me. See, Walter says that if you know what happened before, then you can work to make sure it never comes again, right?"

On the final day of the visit, the entire group assembled at the Jewish cemetery of Bullay. The harvest was a week closer and late summer rains kept the grapes growing and greener than ever. Everyone predicted a good harvest. Over a hundred people had turned out that cloudy afternoon and a cantor had come down from the Bonn synagogue to lead a Kaddish service. Someone provided yarmulkes for the men to wear.

Making her way gingerly toward Ernst was Marie, the child-out-of-wedlock who never abandoned the Kahn family. She walked with a cane, and had for ten years, ever since her stroke. After the war, Marie was not forgotten by the Kahns, and she came to America nearly every holiday and spent it in their homes. "How could we not invite her?" Thea Kahn said. "She was so good to my husband when so few others were."

The Stadtfelds were there. Erna was dressed in white and sported a matching floppy hat. Eleanor in black, wore a prim bonnet. Their brother Hermann had died several years before. Erna sat with Walter and the two busied themselves with stories and memories. School children peered over the picket fence and a young couple, riding through the vineyards on their bicycles, stopped to watch. The cantor said his prayers. Someone added a few words. Afterwards people mingled among the graves. Erna stood before her father's stone, which she had not visited in six decades. With her mouth set firm, she went and broke off a small branch and dusted off her father's stone. "My mother doesn't have one," she said quietly.

Cantor introducing memorial service in the Bullay Jewish cemetery. Walter and Ernst Kahn are seated.

Lee stood before Max Wolf's tomb. "Terrible about his suicide," she said shaking her head, as if it had just happened. Angelika helped Walter out of his chair and the two of them made their way slowly over the freshly cut grass to the far end of the cemetery. There Walter stood before the grave of Josef Sondheimer, then he paid his respects to Moses and Adam and Julius. Angelika helped Walter back up the hill. I took a final picture and headed out of the cemetery toward the car. Gerda was standing there alone, gazing over the hills, the vineyards, the river.

"So how was it for you Gerda? How was this visit home?" I asked as I laid my camera bag on the back seat of my car. Gerda smiled. "Don't you worry. I'll be back for the harvest." Then she looked away from me and returned to her memories.

I started up the car and made my way through the poky tourist traffic of Zell, headed over the Hunsrück and picked up the autobahn for Mainz and Frankfurt. I turned north and shot toward Berlin. I arrived after midnight. A week later, with film developed and contact sheets before me to jog my memory, I began typing out my notes. A few weeks later Angelika wrote to tell me that Walter Kahn had died in a Florida hospital and his brother Hans had died a week later. I phoned Ernst in Boca Raton, Florida to express my condolences and wrote a letter to Hannes Schmit in Wittlich and told him how sorry I was to hear that his friend Walter was dead.

Cochem high school students posing questions to former Jewish residents of the Mosel. September 1995.

To Sachsenhausen
with Israelis. January 1996

Another concentration camp, another press bus. It had been six years and two months since that trip to Auschwitz with the German press corps, which spun this project into motion. Now I was heading for Sachsenhausen with Israeli journalists, accompanying Israel's President Ezer Weizman on his first official visit to Germany.

When I began thinking of this book in 1989, there were two German states, communism controlled Central Europe, Saddam Hussein was eyeing Kuwait, and Israel's relations with the Arab states (except Egypt) were still hostile. Most of that has been radically rewritten. The world is a vastly different place.

Roman Herzog, Germany's president, accompanied his Jewish counterpart through the Sachsenhausen concentration camp near Berlin, and to the site of the crematoria there. Diplomats and dignitaries flanked the two heads of state as they walked over the camp grounds. Silence prevailed save for the crunch of footsteps on gravel, the whir and click of the cameras that moved with them.

Around 10,000 Jews died in this brutal work camp and Weizman had come to pay his respects at the site their corpses were burned. As a bitter wind blew down from the north, the seventy-seven year old cantor serving Berlin's Pestalozzistrasse synagogue, Estrongo Nachama, moved out before the assembled and prepared to recite Kaddish. The old man had been waiting in the cold for nearly an hour, but just as he was about to begin, Weizman suddenly asked where he was from. Nachama, not quite comprehending, looked around, leaned toward the Israeli and said quietly, "Auschwitz."

It hurt to hear it. Estrongo Nachama was born in Salonika and grew up in Greece until the Nazis took him and his family away. He survived, they did not. When World War Two ended, Nachama, who had been shunted from one camp to another by the SS, had also been at this very place: Sachsenhausen. With no reason to return home to Greece, he wandered, staggered into devastated Berlin, was cared for by Jews there, and ended up staying. Ezer Weizman and Estrongo Nachama looked at each other for a brief moment, then the cantor began his service. Television lights glared, microphones stretched out, cameras clicked.

Judaism is based on memory. Descendants of Jews expelled from Spain five hundred years ago still keep the keys their forbears brought with them from Castille and Aragon. But it is more than just memory; this is collective memory and it runs deep in the Jew. The tragedy of fifty years ago, the greatest that befell the Jewish people in the past 2,000 years, will remain fresh and painful for generations to come.

But if Judaism is built on remembering, postwar Germany, founded at what Germans call *Stunde Null*, zero hour, means the opposite. Remembering is not something a great many Germans wish to do, or can do, very comfortably. More than a few hate even being reminded of the Third Reich. Yet since the late 1970s, German society has slowly become engaged in exploring its ugly past. It is uneven and awkward, to be sure, but the process goes on and it cannot stop. This exploration is now part of the national psyche. Oddly enough, just like

Cantor Estrongo Nachama donning his robes before a memorial service at Dachau concentration camp. May 1993.

the old expression that says "When you forget you're Jew, the world will remind you," so it seems to apply for Germans born after the war. They cannot escape the past. *Stunde Null* in this matter, hasn't even started and that is a painful thing for young Germans to come to terms with.

Jews live in Germany. Not all are wholly comfortable here, but with a continuing influx of Jews from the former Soviet Union, a Jewish presence will remain on German soil for years to come. No one thought it would happen but it has. More than a few of their neighbors don't know what to make of them; there are Jews the world over who cannot forgive them for being here at all, and I cannot help but feel this is too heavy a load for 50,000 Jews to bear.

In the decade I have devoted to observing contemporary Jewish life in Central Europe and the Balkans, I remember most the scenes that didn't fit my own preconceived ideas. In Romania in 1987, a Jewish butcher who worked four days a week to provide kosher meat for thirty familes in five rural counties told me: numbers don't count. In Bosnia in 1993, I watched as Sarajevo's Holocaust survivors and their offspring turned a synagogue into a non-sectarian aid agency.

This is the unexpected memory I carry of Germany: It was a grey Sunday evening in Berlin in 1995 at the close of a youth seminar for newly-arrived Jewish teenagers from the former Soviet Union. Sixty youngsters attended. One teenage girl, who had to hurry to catch the train that would bring her back to the barracks in which she was living outside Erfurt, ran over to Deni Kranz, the program organizer. "I just want to thank you for inviting me," she said breathlessly as she grabbed his hands in both of hers. Looking into his eyes, she said, "Really. For the first time in my life, I feel Jewish. So thanks!" With that she kissed his cheeks, grabbed her backpack and hurried out the door. I

Israeli President Ezer Weizman speaking with Cantor Estrongo Nachama at the Sachsenhausen concentration camp. January 1996.

took a camera and chased after her down Oranienburger Strasse, wondering if I might shoot a usable picture.

When I first set foot on this street one rainy November morning in 1988, it was lifeless and boarded-up and grim. On this day, nearly eight years later, the girl ran past the Jewish community center where people were filing inside for a lecture, then the entrance to the Centrum Judaicum Museum, next to a crowded restaurant run by Israelis, and the Jewish community's art gallery. She vanished into the subway. No picture in that for me. But I smiled thinking over what she had just said and I rolled it around in my head. The Russian girl just thanked someone for helping her feel Jewish in Germany. Not for the first time in Central Europe, I felt the wheels of history turning.

Acknowledgements

I am deeply beholden to all those who helped bring this project to fruition and I begin with two who helped guide me from the beginning, Rabbi Andrew Baker of the American Jewish Committee and Dr Andreas Nachama of Jewish Cultural Days—Berlin.

Much of this work was done while on assignment for the Central Welfare Council of Jews in Germany, and three colleagues there, Bennie Bloch, Aviva Goldschmidt and Deni Kranz, opened all doors for me. An early exhibition of that work was shown at the Jüdisches Museum der Stadt Frankfurt, and I thank curator Cilly Kugelmann and Georg Heuberger, the museum's director.

The entire Mosel River chapter happened only because Angelika Schleindel spent a great deal of time with me while I was there, then read and corrected my drafts.

In the Jewish communities around Germany, special thanks to Michael Szentei-Heise of Düsseldorf and Stefan Szajak of Frankfurt.

Some of these pictures were taken on assignment for *TIME Magazine*, the *London Independent*, *Wochenpost*, *Die Zeit*, the *Philadelphia Inquirer Magazine*, the *London Guardian Magazine* and the *Washington Post*.

I also would like to thank the following: Helmut Braun of the Berlin Jewish Museum, Julius H. Schoeps of the Moses Mendelssohn Center in Potsdam, Werner Perger of *Die Zeit*, Norma Drimmer of the Berlin Jewish community, Paul Spiegel and especially Hermann Simon of the Centrum Judaicum Museum.

I also appreciate the suggestions, aid and advocacy of Rabbi Rodney Mariner in London, Dieter Dettke of the Friedrich-Ebert-Foundation's Washington office, Wolfgang Gibowski of the Federal Press and Information Agency, Stefan Eisel of the Konrad Adenauer Foundation and Jürgen Wickert of the Friedrich Naumann Foundation.

My assistant, Regine Wosnitza did an enormous amount of research and combed through my German translation and Vera Stutz-Bischitzky also made suggestions for the translation. Karsten Schirmer did all the photographic printing.

I greatly appreciate the support of *Leica* Cameras, GmbH. At *Nicolai*, thanks to editors Carolin Hilker-Siebenhaar and Antonia Meiners, and to publisher Thomas Karlauf. I am also indebted to as Reinhard Koester, who designed the book.

Special thanks to my text editor, Deborah Unger, and my agent, Thomas Schlueck. Once again, thanks to Ruth Gruber for reading the text at every stage and making invaluable suggestions.

Johann Strauss
(Sohn)

Der Zigeuner-baron

Gesamtaufnahme

Grace Bumbry · Rita Streich
Biserka Cvejic · Gisela Litz
Nicolai Gedda · Kurt Böhme
Hermann Prey · Willi Brokmeier
Wolfgang Anheisser
Chor und Orchester der
Bayerischen Staatsoper
München
Franz Allers